AS/A-LEVEL YEAR 1

STUDENT GUIDE

SET TEXT BO

WJEC/Eduqas

Business

Business functions

Mark Hage

Tracey Bell

HODDER
EDUCATION
AN HACHETTE UK COMPANY

Hodder Education, an Hachette UK company, Blenheim Court, George Street, Banbury, Oxfordshire OX16 5BH

Orders

Bookpoint Ltd, 130 Park Drive, Milton Park, Abingdon, Oxfordshire OX14 4SB

tel: 01235 827720

fax: 01235 400401

e-mail: education@bookpoint.co.uk

Lines are open 9.00 a.m.–5.00 p.m., Monday to Saturday, with a 24-hour message answering service. You can also order through the Hodder Education website: www.hoddereducation.co.uk

© Mark Hage and Tracey Bell 2018

ISBN 978-1-5104-1987-2

First printed 2018

Impression number 5 4 3 2

Year 2022 2021 2020 2019

This Guide has been written specifically to support students preparing for the WJEC/Eduqas AS and A-level Business examinations. The content has been neither approved nor endorsed by WJEC/Eduqas and remains the sole responsibility of the authors.

Cover photograph: Sashkin/Shutterstock

Typeset by Integra Software Services Pvt. Ltd., Pondicherry, India

Printed in India

Hachette UK's policy is to use papers that are natural, renewable and recyclable products and made from wood grown in sustainable forests. The logging and manufacturing processes are expected to conform to the environmental regulations of the country of origin.

Contents

Getting the most from this book 4

About this book 5

Content Guidance

Marketing 6

Finance 21

People in organisations (human resources) 30

Operations management 48

Questions & Answers

1 WJEC AS

Operating profit 63

Financial and non-financial methods of motivation 64

Distribution channels 66

2 WJEC Eduqas AS

Diseconomies of scale 69

Management by objectives 70

Labour turnover 72

3 WJEC Eduqas A-level

Added value 75

Stock control 76

Waste 79

Knowledge check answers 82

Index 83

▌Getting the most from this book

Exam tips

Advice on key points in the text to help you learn and recall content, avoid pitfalls, and polish your exam technique in order to boost your grade.

Knowledge check

Rapid-fire questions throughout the Content Guidance section to check your understanding.

Knowledge check answers

1 Turn to the back of the book for the Knowledge check answers.

Summaries

■ Each core topic is rounded off by a bullet-list summary for quick-check reference of what you need to know.

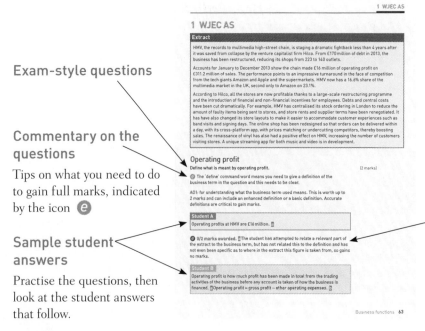

Exam-style questions

Commentary on the questions

Tips on what you need to do to gain full marks, indicated by the icon ⓔ

Sample student answers

Practise the questions, then look at the student answers that follow.

Commentary on sample student answers

Read the comments (preceded by the icon ⓔ) showing how many marks each answer would be awarded in the exam and exactly where marks are gained or lost.

◼ About this book

This guide has been written with one thing in mind: to provide you with the ideal resource for your revision of both the WJEC Business AS and the first year of the WJEC Eduqas Business A-level.

In your study of the subject you will look at business in a variety of contexts, small and large, national and global, service and manufacturing. This book covers the theme of Unit 2/Component 1: Business functions.

The **Content Guidance** section offers concise coverage, combining an overview of key terms and concepts with identification of opportunities for you to illustrate higher level skills of analysis and evaluation.

The **Questions & Answers** section provides examples of stimulus materials and the various types of questions that you are likely to face: both short-answer and data response questions. The questions cover both WJEC AS and WJEC Eduqas AS and A-level Business. They also give explanations of command words which can be applied to any question with the same word. The answers are also explained in detail including the grades obtained.

A common problem for students and teachers is the lack of resources and in particular exam-style questions that cover individual areas of study. The questions in this guide are tailored so you can apply your learning while the topic is still fresh in your mind, either during the course itself or when you have revised a topic in preparation for the examination. Along with the sample answers this should provide you with a sound basis for sitting your exams in Business.

Pre-existing knowledge

AS and A-level Business presumes students have no specific previous experience of the subject. The good news is everyone starts at the very beginning in terms of the key terms and knowledge. The most important attribute at this stage is an interest in current news about businesses you are familiar with, such as Apple and McDonald's. Business is a subject that requires you to apply key terms to real businesses so an interest in businesses in the news will help you significantly to contextualise the theories. This is the really enjoyable part of the subject, and will assist you towards scoring highly in the exam.

Content Guidance

■ Marketing

Marketing involves identifying, predicting and satisfying customer needs in order to create a competitive advantage and allow a business to make a greater profit.

Marketing's purpose is to:
- identify and analyse, by using market research, new products for current markets and new markets
- satisfy customer needs so that loyalty to the product and/or brand means repeat purchasers

Marketing is vitally important to different types of business organisation. Larger businesses will dedicate specific staff and departments to it, while smaller ones may need or choose to contract the tasks to specialist businesses. Marketing matters to businesses because:
- it increases customers' awareness of products and therefore influences sales
- operations will need to use sales forecasts produced by the marketing department to plan their production schedules and staffing requirements

Product orientation

Product orientation means that a business focuses primarily on creating and developing a high-quality good or service — but perhaps ignores customer preferences and priorities.

Market orientation

Market orientation means that a business chooses to design a product or service to meet the requirements of customers' desires or needs. Market research is critical to the success of a market-orientated business as it offers many different methods of identifying customers' tastes and priorities.

Asset-led marketing

Asset-led marketing is where the qualities of the business and its products (known as the assets) are used to meet customer needs. Asset-led marketing tries to utilise the internal strengths of the business, such as a skilled workforce or the use of technology, to satisfy customers' requirements.

The marketing mix

The term **marketing mix** means the way in which a business controls four elements, called the four Ps, to ensure the product is suitable for potential customers. The four Ps include product, price, place and promotion as shown in Figure 1.

Marketing The process of identifying, predicting and satisfying customer needs in order to make a profit.

Market orientation Where a business aims to provide a product or service to meet customers' wants or needs.

Asset-led marketing An approach whereby a business's assets (the qualities of the business and its products) are used to meet customer needs.

Knowledge check 1

Give one reason why Marks and Spencer's use of asset-led marketing may not be improving the sales of its clothing.

Marketing mix The way a business controls the four Ps: product, price, place and promotion.

Figure 1 The four Ps of the marketing mix

The secret of a successful marketing mix is ensuring that it is well integrated across the four elements, and that the whole mix creates the right image to match the marketing opportunity that has been identified.

Product

Product means the object or service that is offered for sale to the customer. A product can be as simple as an apple or as sophisticated as an aircraft.

A **product portfolio** is the term given to the full range of products and brands produced by a business. For example, the online shopping channel QVC has over 15,000 items in its current product portfolio.

Brand

A **brand** is a name, symbol or design for a product or service which attempts to make it unique, differentiating it from competitors' products or services.

The main way to build a brand is by focusing on a **unique selling point (USP)**, something about the product that makes it different from other products on the market.

Product differentiation

Product differentiation refers to actual or perceived features of a product or service which a business uses to convince customers to buy its product or service instead of competitors'.

An advantage of production differentiation is that a business focuses on telling customers what is different and better about the product, which can **add value**, making customers willing to pay a higher price.

A disadvantage is that the attempt to be different might add more to the design and production costs than customers are willing to pay.

> **Exam tip**
>
> Use concepts such as competitive advantage to help evaluate a business's strengths within its market. And don't define a differentiated product simply as one that is different as this will gain no marks.

Product portfolio The full range of products and brands produced by a business.

Brand A name, symbol or design which differentiates a product or service from others in the market.

Unique selling point An aspect of a product that clearly differentiates it from other, similar products.

Added value The difference between the price of the finished product or service and the cost of bought-in goods and services. The more exciting and original the features of the product, the higher the value may be to the customer.

The importance to a business and its stakeholders of having the right product

In order for a business to have the right products it will need to take into account:

- **Its own strengths and weaknesses**. For example, innovative businesses such as Apple will have the personnel and infrastructure to create new technologies.
- **Competition** from other businesses both in terms of market share and perceived technical and financial capabilities.
- **Stakeholders such as shareholders** who will not wish to take large financial risks with new products unless it can be shown that the business has the capabilities to make a profit from them. Employees will also want to be sure that any venture into new products has been well thought through, with the relevant financial backing. The business will need to show that potential customers are willing to purchase a new product in sufficient numbers and at a price that makes the business a profit.

To ensure that a product meets the needs of the target market, an effective **design mix** is needed, consisting of the product's function, aesthetics (looks) and the costs of creating and manufacturing it:

- **Function** is how effectively the product works: does a smartphone have great sound, a brilliant camera and long battery life? Is it reliable?
- **Aesthetics** are how the product appeals to customers in terms of how it looks, feels or smells. This can differentiate the product from others in the same market, creating more customer demand.
- **Costs of creating the product** include the costs involved in its manufacture and production. The product must be designed so it can be produced cheaply enough to make a profit.

To ensure the product achieves the maximum profits for the business the design mix may need to be adapted to reflect:

- **Social trends:** the cultural values and practices of customers.
- **Concern over resource depletion:** if a raw material used in the manufacturing process is becoming rarer, the business may want to redesign the product to do without this material.
- **Concern over waste management:** the design mix should focus on reducing the use of raw materials and energy in the production of the product.
- **Ethical sourcing:** taking into account ethical issues when sourcing materials. This might include issues such as the pay and working conditions of the workforce producing the materials, as well as issues such as sustainability.

The product life cycle

The **product life cycle** describes the stages a product goes through from its very beginnings until its final removal from the market. Not all products reach this final stage. Some continue to grow and others rise and fall.

The main stages of the product life cycle are:

- **Introduction:** the research, development and then launch of the product.
- **Growth:** when sales are increasing at their fastest rate.

Design mix The combination of the three factors needed to create an effective product: function, aesthetics and the costs of making it.

Exam tip

You should be able to identify and evaluate which aspect of the product and its stakeholders is relevant to a question. Remember that there are always downsides to differentiated products such as extra costs, so also look at the bigger picture.

Knowledge check 2

Out of the three design mix factors, which one or two might be the priorities for:

(a) Boeing and its new near-supersonic passenger jet?

(b) Gucci and its new £4,000 handbag?

(c) Barratt Homes, with its new starter homes for inner London?

Product life cycle The stages a product goes through from initial conception to eventual removal from the market.

- **Maturity:** when sales are near their highest, but the rate of growth is slowing down.
- **Saturation:** when everyone who might want the product has got it.
- **Decline:** the final stage of the cycle, when sales begin to fall.

How to construct a product life cycle diagram including extension strategies

- First draw the two axes, with sales on the vertical axis and time on the horizontal axis. Make sure you annotate them correctly.
- Next split the horizontal axis into introduction, growth, maturity, saturation and decline, as shown in Figure 2.
- Finally, draw a line charting the development and decline of the product on the graph. Products follow a similar pattern unless they fail to make any sales, in which case there will be little growth after the introduction stage and a shorter drop to the decline stage.
- The effect of an extension strategy can be drawn by adding a line going up from the end of the maturity stage, as shown on Figure 2. This shows that the strategy has extended the number of sales compared to the decline that would have taken place without any action by the business.

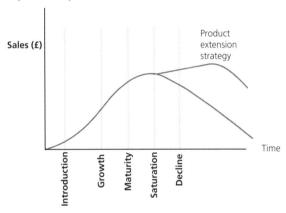

Figure 2 Product life cycle with an extension strategy

Evaluating the impact of extension strategies

The business can find out at what point the product is in its life cycle by looking at the sales of the product compared with previous sales. As products cost a lot of money to design and manufacture, businesses attempt to recoup their costs by keeping sales as high as possible through **extension strategies**, such as:

- Reformulating the product, to position it more clearly towards a slightly different market.
- Changing the promotional focus, such as when the advertising for Johnson's Baby Powder switched from babies to mums.

The impact of the extension strategy will depend on a number of factors including:

- **Competitors:** if other businesses have already introduced new products then these may offset the effectiveness of an extension strategy.

- **Customers:** if customers are loyal to the product then an extension strategy is likely to be more effective.
- **The age of the product:** if the product is significantly outdated in terms of its looks or technical abilities then an extension strategy is likely to have little effect on improving sales and stopping its decline.

The problem for a business is that all these factors are difficult to judge. Regular market research will assist the business in knowing when to introduce an extension strategy and what that strategy should be.

The relationship between the product life cycle and cash flow

Referring back to Figure 2, the cash flow in the different stages is:
- **Introduction:** a significant amount of cash will have been spent on the development and promotion of the product with little money returned in sales. Cash flow will be negative at this stage.
- **Growth:** spending is still high in terms of promoting the product as it is new to the market. However, sales are starting to increase so at some point in the growth stage, cash flow will start to become positive. Remember, the product is unlikely to have made a profit at this stage.
- **Maturity:** much less money will be spent on promotion and sales will be at their peak, with positive cash flow into the business.
- **Decline:** cash flow into the business will be declining as sales start to drop off. The business will need to decide at what point it should cease selling the product.
- **Extension strategy:** this is likely to include a greater cash flow out of the business for more promotion and/or enhanced features added to the product.

Product life cycles for different businesses, products and markets

Table 1 Examples of product life cycles for different businesses, products and markets

	Product life cycle	Extension strategies
Businesses	**Manufacturing:** long introduction stage due to time spent on developing the product. Growth and maturity stages have a relatively long lifetime, particularly for drugs such as cancer treatments. **Retailers:** short introduction stage as products are already available for sale. Growth will feature heavy promotion and have a relatively short time span. Maturity will last for a relatively short period of time ending in decline due to new product launches.	Tend to focus on enhancing the current product by adding new features. Focus heavily on promotion such as price reductions.
Products and markets	**Cars** tend to follow the product life cycle described for manufacturers in a mass market with a great deal of time spent developing and then introducing the product. Growth happens over a period of time with maturity lasting for 2+ years. Decline will happen relatively slowly. **Mobile phones** in a mass market tend to have short product life cycles with short development times and a rapid introduction through large amounts of promotion. Growth happens very quickly with the product reaching maturity and being kept there through further promotion. Decline takes place very quickly.	A combination of additional features and promotion through discounts. Developing new uses of the product. Discounts or targeting a new market segment.

Knowledge check 3

Which type of strategy related to the product life cycle has been adapted for the Apple iPhone 5s?

Evaluating the benefits of the product life cycle to a business and its stakeholders

The advantages of using the product life cycle are:

- **It helps businesses to plan** to ensure there are always products at different stages of the life cycle, so that as one declines another takes its place.
- **It allows stakeholders such as owners and shareholders to be given data** on the different products a business has in the market and in development, to ensure the return on their investment is consistently being met.

The disadvantages include:

- **Difficulties in predicting** which stage a product is at, for example some products may show a decline in sales, but this may only be temporary.
- **Changes in consumer tastes**, which can mean a product life cycle is much shorter than first planned for. Shareholders and investors will have spent a large amount of money developing a product which now becomes a waste and a potential loss.
- **The process is costly** if the business has a lot of products.

Ultimately the product life cycle is a useful tool for businesses and stakeholders, but it should not be relied upon too heavily for a product's ultimate success in the market.

The Boston matrix

A business's product portfolio can be analysed using the **Boston matrix** which can help a business to decide on its spending priorities regarding product development and promotion. The Boston matrix places products into one of four different categories, based on whether the product:

- has a high or low market share
- is in a sector with high or low market growth

Boston matrix Analyses a company's product portfolio in relation to the rate of market growth and the level of market share.

Figure 3 shows the four different categories: cash cow, rising star, problem child and dog

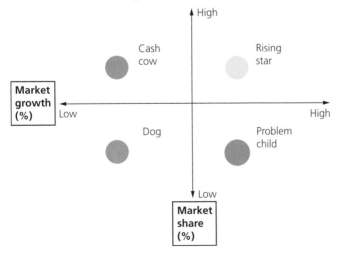

Figure 3 The Boston matrix

The four categories of the Boston matrix:

- **Cash cows** are low-growth mature products with a high market share and little need for investment.
- **Rising stars** have a strong share of a high-growth market making them hugely valuable, profitable today and potentially even more so in the future.
- **Problem children** are products with a low market share operating in a high-growth market. They may have potential if the right investment is put behind them.
- **Dogs** are products with a low market share in low-growth markets. They may generate enough cash to be worth continuing selling, but are rarely worth investing in.

The Boston matrix is used to decide how to allocate marketing resources. Instead of spending equally on all products, a business might 'milk' its cows to provide the cash to support its rising stars and problem children.

Evaluating the use of the Boston matrix to a business and its stakeholders

Benefits include helping the business to analyse its product portfolio to see which products may be able to generate the greatest sales revenue, which can then be used to help other products such as a problem child.

Drawbacks include its inability to predict how products might perform in the future, risking a business wasting money, for example on marketing.

Price

Price is the amount the business charges the customer for the product or service. A business can work out the price it will sell its product at by looking at factors including the costs of producing the product, its brand image, the target market and the target customers. This will help the business form a pricing strategy.

Different strategies used to determine the appropriate price

- **Cost-plus pricing** is where the business adds together the raw material, labour and overhead costs for a product. This gives the cost per unit, also known as unit cost. The business then adds to it a mark-up percentage (to create a profit margin) in order to create the price of the product. Benefits of cost-plus pricing are that it is easy to calculate and price increases can be justified when costs increase. However, it ignores price elasticity of demand and how sensitive the product is to rises in price.
- **Price skimming** means the business sets a high price before other competitors come into the market or when the new product is believed to be superior to others on the market. Benefits include allowing for greater profit from customers prepared to pay the premium price, often called 'early adopters'. However, sometimes the strategy breaks down as other competitors enter the market.
- **Penetration pricing** means the business sets a relatively low initial price to attract new customers. Benefits include encouraging customers to switch to the new product to achieve a high market share. However, profit levels are likely to be low, making it hard for the product to establish a quality reputation.

> **Exam tip**
>
> Like all models, the Boston matrix simplifies a complex world. Cadbury could treat its Dairy Milk brand as a cash cow, but experience teaches it that the brand still benefits from investment rather than simply being 'milked'.

> **Knowledge check 4**
>
> Why should a business see the Boston matrix as a tool to aid planning rather than as a predictor of successful products?

Price skimming Setting a high price before other competitors come into the market.

Penetration pricing Setting a relatively low initial price — usually lower than the intended established price — to attract new customers.

- **Competitive pricing** means the business must accept the going market price and be a 'price taker'. A benefit is that it avoids price competition, allowing the business to compete in other ways such as through promotion. A drawback is that the price adopted may be so low it does not cover the production costs.
- **Psychological pricing** means the price is intended to make the customer believe that the product is cheaper than it really is, e.g. £9.99 instead of £10. Benefits include the perception that customers are getting good value for money, encouraging greater sales revenue. However, customers may see this as simply a marketing gimmick and lose trust in the business.
- **Contribution pricing** means setting a price based on the variable costs of making or purchasing the product and trying to make sure that the selling price covers the fixed costs of the business. The benefit is that the contribution made, which is higher than the variable and fixed costs per unit, will mean the business is not only covering its breakeven point but is able to achieve a profit. However, the price set may be much higher than those of competitors, meaning products are unlikely to sell.

How different types of business organisations use different pricing strategies

There are many factors a business must take into account when choosing the most appropriate pricing strategy:

- **Unique selling point (USP):** a product with a USP is differentiated from the rest of the market.
- **Price elasticity of demand.**
- **Level of competition:** if there are many similar products then competitive pricing will be needed.
- **Strength of brand:** if the business has a well-established and positive image its products are likely to command a premium price.
- **The stage in the product life cycle:** if the product is relatively new and innovative, price skimming may be adopted to gain maximum profit. Later on, the business may need to switch to a competitive pricing approach.
- **Costs and the need to make a profit:** if the business's key priority is to ensure that a profit is made from each sale, then cost-plus pricing may need to be used.
- **Online sales and the growth of price comparison websites** have made it easy for customers to compare the prices of a product sold through a variety of online and physical stores. This means having an online price based on competitive pricing.

Evaluating the importance of selecting the most appropriate pricing strategy

Selecting the right pricing strategy is important because:

- Pricing is a vital ingredient in customers' decisions whether or not to purchase the product.
- The business needs to find out how much the target market is willing to pay.

Competitive pricing
Where the forces of demand and supply or competition from similar products mean that a business must accept the going market price.

Psychological pricing
The price is set to make the customer believe the product is cheaper than it really is.

Contribution pricing
Pricing based on the variable costs of making or purchasing the product, intended to make sure the selling price covers the fixed costs of the business.

Exam tip

Terminology is important. If you can distinguish clearly between the different pricing methods, you will be able to write far stronger arguments.

Knowledge check 5

Why might a new competitor to Apple's smartphone, Huawei, have to charge less than Apple for their similarly specified phone?

The business should also pay careful attention to where the product is in its life cycle when choosing a pricing strategy. For example, a business launching a new product such as a television is likely to adopt a price skimming strategy to attract early adopters.

However, the business may have to adopt a strategy such as cost-plus pricing in order for it to survive, so may in fact have few options. Instead such businesses will concentrate on product differentiation, promotion and customer service to help with sales.

Promotion

Promotion is the way a business makes its products known to its current and potential customers. It involves communicating with customers about the product and persuading them to purchase it through a combination of methods, called the **promotional mix**.

Which promotional methods are used depends on factors such as how long the product has been on sale, what the product is, competition and the target market.

Promotion can be classified in the following ways:

■ **Above-the-line promotion** which is communication that is paid for, such as advertising on television, in newspapers or on the internet. It can be aimed at a specific audience but can be viewed by anyone. The aims of above-the-line promotion are to inform customers, raise awareness and build brand positioning. Above-the-line tends to have a higher cost since the promotional methods used are less precise.

■ **Below-the-line promotion**, where the business has direct control over the target or intended audience. There are many methods of below-the-line promotion, including sales promotions such as buy-one-get-one-free, direct marketing, personal selling and sponsorship.

Different types of promotional strategy

Advertising, is used by many businesses large and small. It is done through media such as television, newspapers and social media. Television is expensive and is only useful for products sold in a mass market. Newspaper adverts can be used by small businesses, either in a local paper or in national newspapers. The cost of adverts increases based on the size of advert and whether the audience is local, regional or national. The costs of advertising via the internet using adverts on websites or phone apps will depend on the sophistication of the advert and the size of the market it can potentially reach.

A strength of advertising is that it can target a large audience with prepared messages, encouraging a large increase in sales. A drawback is that national adverts can be extremely expensive and the business will need to spend a large amount of money on a sustained campaign in order to ensure customer engagement and sales.

Viral marketing involves creating advertising that is attention-grabbing for use on social media, with the hope that customers will spread the message. A benefit is that it can be used by small or large businesses with the campaign costing nothing at all. However, campaigns are difficult to create and cannot be repeated, even if successful.

Exam tip

The product life cycle is such an obvious model that few students take it seriously. In fact, it is a great basis for impressive analysis of, for example, different pricing methods at different stages in the life cycle.

Knowledge check 6

What type of brand can adopt a premium price?

Above-the-line promotion Paid-for communication such as advertising on television, in newspapers or on the internet.

Below-the-line promotion Where the business has direct control over the target or intended customers.

Viral marketing Creating memorable and attention-grabbing advertising for use in social media campaigns, with the hope that customers will share the adverts.

Emotional marketing is intended to appeal to the customers' needs and aspirations by focusing on how a product can enhance self-esteem and/or happiness. It can be used by large businesses who can afford to spend money hiring celebrities or sports personalities, or by charitable organisations to encourage financial support for a cause. The benefit is that, as studies have shown, customers' emotional responses are often powerful motivators in their purchasing decisions. However, emotions are difficult to predict and engage, and without a large amount of research and planning this type of marketing may backfire, and the business or product may end up being seen as false and insincere.

Public relations (PR) involves creating and maintaining a positive image of the business and/or product. One method is through **sponsorship**, where a business pays a celebrity or sports team to advertise its products. This can increase brand awareness and promote a positive image. However, sponsorship is an expensive form of promotion so it tends to be used only by large businesses. An example of effective use of sponsorship is Monde Nissin's sponsorship of Mo Farah to be the face of Quorn, a meat substitute product. Sales of Quorn have risen 17% since Farah's sponsorship deal.

> **Exam tip**
>
> Be sceptical of the information provided by companies (including articles from sources such as the *Metro* newspaper or online blogs). Businesses employ PR companies to boost their image, not to tell the whole truth.

Evaluating the impact on a business and its stakeholders of selecting the right promotional strategy

- The right promotional strategy can create and enhance a product and brand image that differentiates it from competitors', allowing growth in market share and the potential to make the products less price elastic.
- Staff and managers will find it much easier to sell products due to high brand loyalty, leading to improvements in staff motivation and pay.
- Shareholders will see an increase in their share values and larger dividends.
- However, a significant investment in planning promotional activities in terms of time, money and resources is critical to encouraging customer purchases and loyalty.

Place

Place, otherwise known as distribution, is about how a business gets its products to its customers. It involves making sure that products are available to customers at the right place and time and in the right quantities.

Distribution channels used by businesses

Distribution channels are ways to get finished products to customers. The main methods of distributing the product are:

- **Producer** to **wholesaler** to **retailer** to customer. The wholesaler buys products in bulk from many producers of goods, storing and breaking them up into small batches for sale to retailers.
- **Producer to retailer to customer.** The producer sells the goods directly to the retailer, missing out the wholesaler, thus avoiding the wholesaler's mark-up.

Emotional marketing
Advertising that aims to appeal to customers' needs and aspirations through their emotions.

Knowledge check 7

Give one example of sponsorship undertaken by a business.

Producer A business that makes, grows, or supplies goods or commodities for sale.

Wholesaler A business that acts as a link between the producer and retailer. It buys in bulk and sells to resellers rather than to customers.

Retailer A business that sells goods or services directly to the customer.

- **Producer to consumer.** The producer sells directly to the customer, missing out both the wholesaler and retailer. This allows the producer to retain all the profits from the sale of its products.
- **Multi-channel distribution**, where a business uses more than one type of distribution channel. For example, Apple sells phones via its website using e-commerce, through its own stores and through retailers such as Carphone Warehouse.

> **Exam tip**
>
> Place (distribution) has sometimes been called the 'silent P' because students underestimate its importance within the mix. Try to link distribution to other elements of the marketing mix when you write your answer.

Evaluating the impact of selecting the right distribution channel for a business

The key to a product's success and a business's ability to maximise its profit is choosing the best distribution channel, taking into account:

- **Customer choice or convenience.** A business may choose a number of distribution methods to maximise the number of customers it sells to.
- **The image a business wishes to create.** For example, a new organic yoghurt might be distributed through independent grocers and upmarket sandwich shops.
- **Social trends.** The buying habits of customers may change and a different distribution channel may be required.
- **Online distribution**, where the move from e-commerce to m-commerce (mobile commerce using smartphones) is threatening high-street chains.
- **Changes from product to service.** For example, advances in technology could mean that customers no longer wish to purchase a physical item such as a CD, but gain delivery of their music by a digital download service such as Spotify or iTunes.

Decisions about the marketing mix

The importance of global marketing and global brands

A **brand** is the marketing practice of creating a name, symbol or design that identifies a product and differentiates it from others. The process involves creating a unique image for a product in the customer's mind, mainly through advertising campaigns with a consistent theme.

The main types of branding are:

- **Product**, where the item has a unique logo or packaging which customers are familiar with, such as the Adidas logo.
- **Personal**, where the product is associated with a celebrity or sports personality who endows the product with the positive values this person symbolises for the target market.
- **Corporate**, where the business advertises a broad range of positive images about itself in the hope that the products will be seen to have the same virtues.

To enhance a brand and ensure it remains relevant to customers, a business must ensure that any promotion reflects current social trends. Social media can be used to try to build a connection between the business and the consumer. Companies such as the milkshake business Shakeaway pay a lot of attention to their Facebook pages and blogs, encouraging customers to suggest new flavours and taking care to answer points and queries.

If a product has a USP and a strong brand image, the business may be able to charge premium prices. Reduced elasticity of demand may also mean the strength of the brand may make customers less sensitive to price increases.

Exam tip

When examiners talk about 'building a brand', think about who benefits. Yes, the brand owner does, but what about the consumer who is paying high prices? And what of a new, small company, trying to break into a market dominated by a strong brand? In this context, the word 'benefit' needs careful evaluation.

Marketing strategies explain how the marketing function fits in with a business's overall strategy. **Global marketing** attempts to increase sales through promotion and advertisements to the international market. The right global marketing strategy will find a fit between an individual company's objectives and its unique market position internationally. Table 2 gives examples of business strategies and how these might link with global marketing strategies.

Table 2 Business strategies and thier related global marketing strategies

Business strategy	Example of global marketing strategy
Grow sales	■ Launch new products in different markets ■ Start selling current products into overseas markets
Increase profits	■ Increase selling prices in overseas markets ■ Reduce the amount spent on global advertising
Build customer awareness	■ Invest more in global advertising

Multinational corporations such as Coca-Cola use exactly the same global marketing strategies in each market they operate in, which has the advantage of economies of scale across global markets, called **global brands**. This would be a transnational corporation approach, which is also used by Rolls-Royce cars, for example.

However, businesses have increasingly found that global markets are more sophisticated and competition is more intense so glocalisation has become a preferred approach for many global marketing strategies. Glocalisation means the business thinks globally about its overall marketing strategy but adapts it to meet the needs of the local market. Hence the phrase 'think global, act local'. The most well-known example is McDonald's fast food restaurants which customises its menus and practices to suit local tastes in different countries.

Knowledge check 8

How does Nike's sponsorship of sports personalities such as the footballer Cristiano Ronaldo allow it to add value to its range of sports wear?

Marketing strategy How the marketing function contributes to the main strategic goals of a business.

Global marketing A strategy that aims to increase sales by marketing products or services internationally.

How the marketing mix will differ in different contexts

The key elements of the marketing mix will differ in different contexts. Table 3 gives some examples to explain how.

Table 3 Examples of how the marketing mix will differ in different contexts

Business context	The marketing mix	Evaluation of the marketing mix
Small, local business	**Product** — targeted at local market needs such as food or commodities, e.g. pet supplies. **Price** — competitive if there are many competitors, such as newsagents, or price skimming for niche products. **Place** — through local distribution such as shops. **Promotion** — adverts in local newspapers, on local radio or on Facebook, or word of mouth.	**Advantages** — costs are kept low. **Disadvantages** — potential for growth in sales and market share is limited, meaning comparatively limited profits.
Large, national business	**Product** — aimed at a large range of customers across a diverse social and geographical range, e.g. petrol. **Price** — depends on the current position in the product life cycle, e.g. a mature product such as petrol would adopt competitive pricing. **Place** — physical locations where the greatest number of customers are found, e.g. petrol stations on busy roads. **Promotion** — heavy use of advertising through television and national newspapers to ensure audience awareness is maintained.	**Advantages** — attracts the greatest number of customers, maximising market share and growth and ultimately profits. **Disadvantages** — competition may be fierce so differentiation on price may not be possible unless products have USPs customers are willing to pay extra for.
Large, global business	**Product** — may have been glocalised unless it is one that has features that span cultural and political barriers, such as Coca-Cola. **Price** — may vary across borders for the same product, e.g. 99¢ for a song on iTunes in the USA compared to the higher price of 99p in the UK. If the market is new and expanding the business could operate price skimming. **Place** — in the main centres for potential customer purchases. For online purchases the focus will be on warehousing stock close to populous locations. **Promotion** — advertising through national television and newspapers.	**Advantages** — a homogenous product across many markets will bring large economies of scale, creating a low-cost base. Brand awareness is likely to be high, leading to customer loyalty and repeat purchases. **Disadvantages** — products risk being unfit for purpose in different markets. There is a high risk of diseconomies of scale and restrictive trade practices by governments to safeguard local businesses. Customers may be alienated by poor customer service.
Goods business	**Product** — focus is on the design mix and packaging to ensure differentiation from competitors in terms of features. **Price** — for a novel product or strong brand image price skimming may be adopted. **Place** — emphasis is on ease of access to the target market, e.g. having a car dealership near popular routes or an Amazon warehouse centrally placed for efficient delivery. **Promotion** — strategy will vary for mass and niche market goods.	**Advantages** — for retailers with a physical presence the emphasis will be on the USP of products to allow businesses to charge premium prices and gain high market share over rivals. For e-tailers the emphasis is on the brand image of products at penetration prices, to gain market share. **Disadvantages** — physical goods are difficult and expensive to store in shops, increasing costs. Businesses often have to operate competitor pricing in markets that are competitive, potentially reducing profit margins.

→

Services business	**Product** — emphasis on customer service and customer experience to gain a USP over rivals. **Price** — if the service is widely available, for example music streaming, competitor pricing will be adopted. If the service is seen as unique or highly branded, price skimming will allow for high profit margins. **Place** — for e-tailers access to popular and reliable computer networks are critical to success. For services such as hair and beauty or gyms, the business needs to be sited close to the target audience, especially if it seen as a luxury. **Promotion** — the approach depends on whether the service is for a mass or niche market. Higher spending may be needed for luxury services, to ensure continued customer engagement.	**Advantages** — strong brand image and/or a personal relationship with the customer base may create high levels of customer loyalty, allowing for premium prices and high profit margins. **Disadvantages** — creating and keeping strong brand loyalty means high costs of promotion. If the service has many competitors then innovation together with competitor-based pricing may mean profit margins are low.
Niche market business	**Product** — will be specialised and designed to meet the needs of a smaller segment of a market. **Price** — will be higher than for a mass market product due to a higher cost base and high product differentiation. **Place** — will emphasise the USP of the product. **Promotion** — will focus on the smaller segments of the target market such as specialist magazines or websites. Promotion will aim to emphasise the USP of the product in order to create a more price inelastic product.	**Advantages** — product differentiation will create price inelasticity, meaning profit margins may be high. Customer loyalty is likely to be strong together with steep barriers to entry for potential new competitors. **Disadvantages** — actual market is likely to be comparatively small so overall profits may be likewise. Poor customer service would mean a large decrease in sales.
Mass market business	**Product** — emphasis on product features and cost efficiency as the market is large, probably with many rivals. **Price** — competitor or penetration pricing in order to maintain or increase market share. **Place** — multiple channels of distribution including physical and online access in order to allow for maximum reach of customers. **Promotion** — a discounter such as Aldi will emphasise value and low prices. Others will highlight differentiated products rather than competing on price.	**Advantages** — potential market is large so sales will be high with high levels of revenue. **Disadvantages** — barriers to entry may be relatively low, meaning businesses will need to watch out for new competitors with differentiated products. Profit margins are likely to be comparatively low due to having to adopt competitor pricing, unless the business is a market leader.
Market structure business	**Product** — if a business is selling to another business (b2b) the product will be designed with cost efficiency and the needs of the customer in mind, whereas if it is designed for the end consumer, the emphasis may be on value added features. **Price** — for b2b customers the price will take into account the purchaser's expertise in understanding costs, so may not have as large a profit margin as one designed for the end consumer, where price skimming may operate. **Place** — for b2b customers there will be little need for expensive retail outlets. Instead the focus will be ensuring the product is available at the right time and place. For end consumers, a significant amount of expenditure may be spent on the retail experience. **Promotion** — for b2b customers there will be a focus on trade magazines and websites and the issuing of technical data to support product claims. With end consumers, a wide range of methods will be used to promote sales.	**Advantages** — for b2b, close relationships with customers ensure sales. For end consumers relationships, brand image, unique features of the product and price competitiveness will allow for higher market share and profit margins. **Disadvantages** — for b2b the markets tend to be comparatively small in terms of customers, so any problems with customer relations mean the likely loss of a significant amount of sales and profit. For end consumers, if the market is highly competitive the business will need to innovate regularly and be price competitive, meaning costs will be high and profit margins low.

New technology

New technology used in marketing and its impact on high-street retailers

Marketing makes use of technology in the following ways:

- **Digital media**, including text, graphics, audio and video that can be transmitted across computer networks, such as the latest blockbuster film on the Netflix streaming platform. Adverts are increasingly tailored to the viewing habits of customers both through internet page views and the use of bespoke apps such as Amazon Prime.
- **Social media** which can be used to try to build a connection between the business and the consumer.
- **E-tailing**, short for electronic retailing, is the selling of retail goods on the internet. Advances in technology have changed customers' habits and preferences. For example, many customers would now rather watch a film through a streaming service than buy a DVD. Businesses need to adapt to this type of dynamic market to keep a competitive advantage.
- **M-commerce:** mobile commerce using smartphones. Increasingly goods and services that used to be found on the high street are moving to the smartphone. Businesses can either exclusively run their services through m-commerce or more likely have it as one of many distribution channels aimed at meeting different customers' needs.

Evaluating the impact of new technology on marketing activities of businesses and their stakeholders

New technology has affected marketing activities in a number of ways:

- **Costs** can be significantly reduced in terms of producing advertising campaigns using digital media over a wide range of devices.
- **The potential audience** for marketing campaigns has increased significantly due to the number of people able to access the internet and use e- and m-commerce. Markets are more easily converted to global markets with businesses able to promote products and services globally, particularly those that are electronic such as video or music streaming.
- Technology has helped businesses identify customers' preferences and **buying habits**, allowing them to target customers with tailored promotional offers. For example, Tesco Clubcard gives money-off vouchers based on the spending habits of customers.
- However, businesses have to spend a significant amount of money on mining the data from websites. This requires a **large investment in computers**. Then there is the cost of promotional activities that have to be extremely responsive to changes in buying habits.

Summary

After studying this topic, you should be able to:

- describe marketing and its importance, product and market orientation together with asset-led marketing
- explain and evaluate the key components of the product element of the marketing mix, including brand, product differentiation, the product life cycle and the Boston matrix
- explain and evaluate the key components of price, including different pricing strategies and how a business might go about selecting the most appropriate approach for its situation
- explain and evaluate the key elements of promotion, including above- and below-the-line promotion and different strategies businesses can use to promote their products
- explain and evaluate the key components of place including distribution channels, and how businesses might select the right distribution channels
- explain the importance of global marketing and global brands and how the marketing mix will be different in various contexts
- explain and evaluate the impact of new technology on the marketing mix and customers' buying habits

■ Finance

The **finance department** has the following roles:

- to prepare, keep and maintain financial records for a business, such as the income statement, balance sheet and sales figures
- to analyse the financial performance of the business and help managers understand the business's financial objectives and make the right decisions to achieve them
- to pay creditors and the wages of employees

Budgeting

A **budget** is a financial plan concerning the revenues and costs of a business. In addition to a business's main budget, individual managers may be set budgets that represent their personal target or limit–'My travel budget is £200 a month' means that £200 is the maximum I can spend without having to ask permission from a superior.

Budget A financial plan for the future detailing the revenues and costs of a business.

Purpose of budgets

A budget's main purpose is to help the business meet its financial objectives. Before a budget is made a forecast of sales/revenue and **expenditure** is made for the period it covers.

The business can then make the best use of its finite resources, weighing up the opportunity cost and trade-offs that must be made to decide how to spend its money for the greatest return.

Expenditure The spending on the day-to-day operation of the business.

The benefits of a budget to a business and its stakeholders include:

- It will give all parties a way of looking at predicted business performance and assessing whether the figures used are realistic when considering the objectives to be achieved.
- Actual performance can be measured against the budget, highlighting any areas that may have deviated from the forecast. This allows the business to investigate and rectify problems before it is affected by them in the longer term.

Knowledge check 9

Give a reason why a budget based on past data may be of little use for a newly launched product.

The drawbacks of budgets to a business and its stakeholders include:

- Budgets can be based on imperfect or unrealistic predictions of future costs, meaning the business ends up incurring more costs.
- If the budget predicts greater costs than are actually incurred it may encourage inefficient use of resources, creating lower profit margins than would otherwise be achieved.

Business finance

Finance is the funding required to set up and expand a business. Finance needs to be matched with the short-, medium- and long-term needs of the business.

Sources of finance available to large businesses and their use in different circumstances

Table 4 Short-, medium- and long-term methods of finance with examples of the purposes for which they might be used

	Short term (within a year)	Medium term (1 year onwards but less than 5 years)	Long term (5 years onwards)
Internal sources	■ Retained profits ■ Selling assets **Purpose:** to help solve cash-flow problems or to fund store refurbishments	■ Retained profits ■ Debentures ■ Share issues **Purpose:** to fund capital expenditure such as new machinery or growth in retail outlets	■ Retained profits **Purpose:** to fund large capital investments such as new buildings
External sources	■ Overdrafts ■ Venture capital ■ Leasing ■ Grants ■ Trade credit **Purpose:** to fund cash - flow problems, new equipment or raw materials	■ Bank loans ■ Venture capital ■ Crowd funding ■ Leasing ■ Grants **Purpose:** to fund new machinery, or R&D and launches of new products	■ Bank loans ■ Debentures ■ Peer-to-peer funding ■ Crowd funding ■ Leasing ■ Grants ■ Share capital **Purpose:** to fund takeovers, expansion plans and large capital investments such as new factories or offices

Internal finance: importance and evaluation

Internal finance means funds found inside the business and can be obtained from:

- **The owner's capital:** the money or other capital that the person setting up the business may have saved or otherwise come by. The benefit of using the owner's capital is that there are no interest costs (in contrast with a loan) and there can be flexibility in how quickly it is paid back. However, the owner may not have enough money to finance the business and if the business fails all the capital will be lost.

Exam tip

Even though a budget looks to be the ideal way for a business to plan its expenditure, the examiner will expect you to recognise that ignoring a range of different perspectives may mean a missed opportunity for the business.

Internal finance Funds that come from inside the business.

- **Retained profits:** the profit kept in the business rather than paid out to its owners, for example a limited company may pay shareholders a **dividend**. Using retained profits is cheaper than taking out a loan, and the business has flexibility to decide how much is used and when. However, there is an opportunity cost as the owner or shareholders may want the retained profits as their income.
- **Sales of assets:** items of property owned by a person or business, regarded as having value. A benefit of using the sale of assets is that not only is cash raised but also there are no more costs involved in maintaining that asset. However, businesses don't always have surplus assets to sell and it is a slow process.

External finance: importance and evaluation

External finance means funds found outside the business. Sources might include:
- **Family and friends.** The benefits and risks of using this source are similar to the business owner using their own capital. Additionally, family and friends may want a say or stake in the business.
- **Banks**, which can provide a fixed-term **bank loan** in return for repayment of the amount plus interest. A benefit of taking out a bank loan is that repayments may be spread over a period of time with less impact on cash flow. A drawback is that the bank will require proof that the business can repay the debt, and there may be a high interest rate.
- **Peer-to-peer funding**, which means lending money to businesses ('peers') without going through a bank or other financial institution. The benefit of using this method of finance is that interest rates tend to be much lower than the rates the banks offer. However, it is more difficult to gain this type of funding as lenders are much more careful about who they lend to.
- **Business angels** who are wealthy, entrepreneurial individuals who provide capital in return for a share in the business, for example shares in a limited company.
- **Crowd funding** where the business raises many small amounts of money from a large number of people. A benefit of this source of finance is that smaller investors are more likely to take risks. However, the business will have to market its idea to investors very effectively, and if the project fails this may damage the reputation of the business.
- **Other businesses.** The benefits and problems are the same as with business angels.

Different sources of finance and their evaluation

- **Loans**: the benefits and risks are discussed above.
- Share capital: funds raised by issuing shares in exchange for cash, a source of finance that is only available to limited companies. The advantage of using share capital is that there are no interest or repayment costs attached to it. However, it is costly and means giving away some of the company and its profits to investors.
- Venture capital: money invested in a business in which there is a significant element of risk, for example a start-up or an expanding company. The benefits are that the money is available quickly and the venture capitalist might also provide business expertise to help make the investment a success. A drawback is that a proportion of the ownership of the business and some of its profits will need to be given to the investor.

Dividend A sum of money paid by a company to its shareholders out of its profits.

Knowledge check 10

When might a business not be able to use retained profit?

Knowledge check 11

Which type of business would be particularly suited to crowd funding?

Exam tip

You need to be able to identify the most appropriate source of finance for the type of business in the given context, making sure you can give reasons for and against its use.

Share capital Funds raised by issuing shares in return for cash.

Venture capital Money invested in a business in which there is a substantial element of risk.

- **Overdraft:** when a bank allows a firm to take out more money than it has in its account. A benefit of an overdraft is that it can be used to cover short-term debts. However, the bank may ask for repayment at any time, and there is a high level of interest charged on this type of loan.
- **Leasing:** a financial facility allowing a business to use an asset such as an industrial robot over a fixed period, in return for regular payments. A benefit of leasing is that the business can pay a relatively small amount of money in the short term for an asset. The problem with leasing is that the business does not own the asset, so it must continue to pay for it, month after month.
- **Trade credit:** where suppliers deliver goods now and are willing to wait for a time before payment, for example 90 days. A benefit of trade credit is that the business does not have to pay for any goods for a period after they have been delivered, allowing it to sell on the goods and make a profit. However, it costs the business to administer the payments and it can only be used for goods supplied and not, for example, to fund expansion.
- **Debt factoring:** where the business sells customer accounts which have outstanding credit to another business to raise cash. This can be a quick method of raising money to enhance cash flow. A disadvantage is that debts are normally sold for less than the amount outstanding, meaning the business does not make as much profit.
- **Grants:** given by charities or the government to help businesses get started, especially in areas of high unemployment. One great benefit is that the business usually doesn't have to pay any of the money back. The difficulty is that grants can be very hard to obtain as many businesses are competing for them.

> **Exam tip**
> Sources of finance need to be looked at in terms of the short, medium and long term when evaluating the extract, especially when completing the 20-mark question.

Cash-flow forecasting

Cash flow is the movement of cash into and out of a business. Cash can flow into a business from many different sources, such as customer payments, loans and money received from investors. Cash can flow out of the business for various reasons, such as payments to suppliers, the payment of wages or taxes and the repayment of bank loans.

A cash-flow forecast is a prediction of cash flowing into and out of the business over a period of time. This allows the business to predict how much net cash flow the business has at any given time.

> **Cash flow** The movement of cash into and out of a business.

> **Cash-flow forecast** A prediction of the amount of cash flowing into and out of the business over a given period of time.

Constructing, calculating and interpreting a cash-flow forecast

To construct a cash-flow forecast:

- First, a list of assumptions about business performance needs to be made, usually based on historical data and market trends.
- Then the anticipated sales for the year, normally prepared month by month, are forecast.
- Next an estimate per month of the cash flow coming into the business from sales is made. See (2) in Table 5 below.
- Then an estimate of cash outflows each month is made. See (3) in Table 5.
- Finally, cash from the start of the month (1) is added and then a calculation is made of the net cash flow that month (4) and the net cash flow at the end of the month (5).

Table 5 Example of a cash-flow forecast

£000s	June	July	August	September	October	November
(1) Cash at start of month	20	25 (6)	20	15	5	10
(2) Cash inflows	25	20	25	20	15	25
(3) Cash outflows	−20	−25	−30	−30	−10	−20
(4) Net cash flow	5	−5	−5	−10	5	5
(5) Cash at end of month	25	20	15	5	10	15

Calculating the cash-flow forecast in Table 5 is completed as follows:

(1) Cash at start of month is the net cash available to the business at the start of each month. For example, June has £20,000.

(2) Cash inflows represent the amount of cash the business receives in that month, for example £25,000 in June.

(3) Cash outflows is the amount of cash the business spends in that month, for example £20,000 in June.

(4) Net cash flow is calculated by taking cash outflows from cash inflows in that month. For example, to work out June's net cash flow:

cash inflow − cash outflow = net cash flow

£25,000 − £20,000 = £5,000

(5) Cash at end of month is calculated by adding the cash at start of month to the net cash flow that month. For example, to work out June's cash at end of month:

cash at start of month + net cash flow for that month = cash at month end

£20,000 + £5,000 = £25,000

(6) The cash at end of month is then taken forward to the next month, for example the cash at end of the month of June, £25,000, becomes the cash at the start of the month of July.

Interpreting the cash flow means analysing the figures to:
- identify potential shortfalls in cash balances in advance
- make sure that the business can afford to pay suppliers and employees
- spot problems with customer payments as the forecast encourages the business to look at how quickly customers are paying their debts
- allow external stakeholders such as banks to see if the business is forecast to meet its financial objectives and take appropriate action if the forecast shows a potential negative cash flow at the end of the month

Evaluating the impact of cash-flow forecasts and ways to improve them

Using a cash-flow forecast can help a business in several ways:
- Identifying a potential shortfall in cash. The business can then seek finance to cover this shortfall.

Knowledge check 12

For a new business why is cash-flow forecasting particularly difficult?

Exam tip

You need to be able to complete and calculate a partially completed cash-flow table for a calculate exam question. As these questions normally carry 4 marks, getting them right can be worth a whole grade.

Exam tip

You need to be able to evaluate a cash-flow forecast in the context of the business. Make sure you use the data provided to inform your judgement and recommendations.

- Comparing actual revenues, costs and profits with how much cash is forecast. The benefit is that the business can find solutions to potential problems.
- Considering whether the business is achieving its **financial objectives** in the business plan. This will allow the business to take any action necessary to achieve these objectives, for example, running an advertising campaign to boost sales.
- Aiding potential investors such as banks and shareholders in making decision about whether to finance the business. This will help investors manage the risk of any investment in terms of the likelihood of being repaid.

Financial objective A goal set by a business which is measured in monetary terms, such as a certain amount of profit to be achieved by a specific date.

Limitations of a cash-flow forecast

The limitations of a cash-flow forecast are that:

- it is not always reliable, largely because assumptions have to be made about the future
- unexpected events such as the 2016 EU membership referendum result may change aspects of the cash inflows or outflows
- for a new business, there may be unexpected costs in production or distribution
- for potential investors, the forecast may be too optimistic and may not take into account unforeseen impacts on sales such as a recession, resulting in investors still losing their money

Exam tip

When evaluating a cash-flow forecast look at the figures and try to assess whether the business has given a realistic prediction of its costs and sales.

The income statement

Profit is the positive gain from an investment or business operation after subtracting all expenses. Profit is important as it can be a source of finance, through retained profit.

Profit can be calculated as follows:

profit = total revenue – total costs

Information on revenue, costs and profits is likely to be prepared and evaluated on a regular basis, particularly in the case of a new business, one that is in financial difficulty or one that is aiming to expand.

The main components of the income statement

An **income statement** is a record of the revenues and costs generated by a business over a specific period (normally 1 year). It shows the profit or loss made by the business.

The main components of the income statement are:

- **The trading account**, which shows the income from sales and the costs of making those sales. It includes the stock held by the business at the start and end of a given period of time, usually a year.
- **The profit and loss account**, which summarises the revenues and costs of the business over a given period of time. Its aim is to show whether the business has made a profit or loss over a financial year.
- **The appropriation account**, which shows what the business has done with any profit made, e.g. the dividends paid to shareholders or the level of retained profit.

Income statement A record of a business's revenues and costs over a specific period, usually 1 year.

The income statement is important because:

- it allows shareholders/owners to see how the business has performed and whether it has made an acceptable profit
- it allows providers of finance to see whether the business is able to generate sufficient profits to remain viable

Looking at the clothing company Ted Baker plc's income statement in Table 6 we can interpret and evaluate its impact as follows:

- The **cost of sales** was under half the money the business made on sales, allowing for a gross profit of £273.1 million. Stakeholders within the business, such as managers and staff, would appear to have sold sufficient products throughout the year through the use of advertising and promotion.
- Cost of sales includes fixed costs such as contracts with suppliers to make products, such as Ted Baker shirts, and variable costs, such as the material needed to create the shirts. Keeping fixed costs low helps reduce the cost of sales.
- Overhead costs are those needed to run the Ted Baker stores and the head office. Keeping these costs as low as possible means operating profit can be high. This will mean taking advantage of cheaper rentals or purchases of shops and looking at innovative ways to deliver the customer experience with more efficient technology.
- Corporation tax is the amount the government taxes each company. In 2017 this was 19% of operating profits. The government as a stakeholder wants to create economic conditions in which businesses can make higher profits, which it can tax in order to pay for the NHS and running of the country in general.
- For stakeholders such as shareholders and senior managers net profit is very important, as the higher the amount, the more return on their share investment they may get from the company.
- To evaluate revenue, costs and profit, the business, shareholders or other stakeholders should not look at a set of financial results in isolation, such as those shown in Table 6.

Cost of sales Those costs that directly generate the sales, including the cost of raw materials, components, goods bought for resale and the direct labour costs.

Table 6 Ted Baker plc's 2016 income statement

Accounting item	Figure (£ms)	Method of calculation	Comment
Revenue	456.2		The value of all the sales made in the financial year
Cost of sales	183.1		The cost of the clothes Ted Baker buys in, which can be variable, and fixed costs
Gross profit	273.1	revenue – cost of sales	
Overheads (costs)	213.8		Cost of running the stores and head office
Operating profit	59.3	gross profit – fixed overheads	
Net financing cost	(0.7)		
Corporation tax	(14.4)		Unlike some, Ted Baker pays taxes
Profit for the year (net profit)	44.2	operating profit – financing and tax	

■ Stakeholders can look at trends to see how a business is performing compared to previous data, normally the previous 12 months. The business should be evaluating its performance on a regular basis, probably daily, to keep costs, revenue and profits in line with expectations. For example, Ted Baker's revenue in 2016 was £456.2 million, higher than the £387 million in 2015, showing a big improvement.

Calculating gross profit and net profit

Gross profit is revenue minus the cost to the business of the products or services being sold. It can be calculated as follows:

gross profit = revenue – cost of sales

Gross profit is important because it needs to be high enough to cover the fixed costs of operating and leave some net profit for shareholders. For example, if a business makes £1,000 revenue from selling its product and its cost of selling those products is £800 the gross profit is:

gross profit = £1,000 – £800

gross profit = £200

Net profit is the amount remaining after all the costs of a business have been subtracted from its revenue. This can be calculated as follows:

net profit = gross profit – total costs

For example, a business has a gross profit of £150 and interest on a loan from the bank of £50 so the net profit would be:

net profit = £150 – £50

net profit = £100

Evaluating ways in which a business could improve its profit

To increase profit, the business can do the following:

■ **Improve sales** by increasing the quantity sold, or increasing the selling price. Higher sales will make better use of production capacity, improving profit margins. However, to increase the quantity sold the business will need to spend more money on promotion of the product and on creating the products to sell.

■ **Reduce variable costs** by reducing the variable costs per unit. This could be done by finding a cheaper supplier or improving production quality so that there is less wastage. However, using a cheaper supplier could risk reducing the quality of the product, which may mean customers become less satisfied with the product and sales actually decline.

■ **Decrease the fixed costs** by cutting administrative or management posts. Cutting unnecessary overheads improves the margin of profit. However, staff cuts can go too far and result in poor customer satisfaction and/or a reduction in quality of product or service.

Gross profit Revenue minus the cost of selling the products or services.

Net profit What is left after all the costs of a business have been taken from its revenues.

Knowledge check 13

If gross profit is £500, cost of sales are £150 and other operating expenses £300, what is the net profit?

Exam tip

You need to be able to compare gross, operating and net profit to evaluate what the figures are saying about the ability of the business to convert sales into profit. Use the extract to work out any problems the business may have, such as high costs of sales.

Knowledge check 14

Why might a business that sells products on credit have poor cash flow?

Ratio analysis

Calculating, interpretating and evaluating gross and net profit margins

Profitability measures profit in relative terms, for example in comparison with revenue. It looks at the capability of a business of earning a profit and can be measured by two calculations: gross profit margin and net profit margin.

Gross profit margin is the calculation used to assess a business's proportion of money left over from revenue after taking into account the cost of goods sold. It is also used to assess the contribution generated by each sale towards covering the fixed overheads of the business. The value of gross profit margin varies from business to business and from industry to industry. The higher the profit margin, the more efficient a company is. Gross profit margin is calculated as follows:

$$\textbf{gross profit margin} = \frac{\text{gross profit}}{\text{revenue}} \times 100$$

For example, if a business makes £1,000 of revenue from selling its product and its gross profit is £200, the gross profit margin would be:

$$\text{gross profit margin} = \frac{£200}{£1,000} \times 100$$

$$\text{gross profit margin} = \quad 20\%$$

The gross profit margin of 20% means that for every £1 generated in sales the business makes 20p to cover costs of sales and other expenses. If the business was a town centre public house selling relatively little food this would be 2% higher than the UK average, which is around 18%. However, if this was a food-led public house the UK industry average rate of profitability is 55%. So, the business would be performing significantly worse than this by 35%.

The benefit of using gross profit margin is that it shows the business and investors how effective it is at selling its products. However, it doesn't include all costs and it is difficult to decide what is a good percentage as the business may have unique features that make it untypical of the industry.

Net profit margin looks at profit after tax as a percentage of sales revenue. It is an important measure of relative profitability as it measures how effective the business is at turning its sales into profit. It also looks at how efficient the business is at maintaining a high operating profit, and how effective it is at adding value during the production process.

$$\textbf{net profit margin} = \frac{\text{net profit}}{\text{revenue}} \times 100$$

For example, if a business has a net profit of £100 and revenue of £1,000, net profit margin is calculated as follows:

$$\text{net profit margin} = \frac{£100}{£1,000} \times 100$$

$$\text{net profit margin} = 10\%$$

Gross profit margin
The calculation used to assess a business's proportion of money left over from revenue after taking into account the cost of goods sold.

Knowledge check 15

Give one reason why pubs that sell food have higher gross profit margins than those that do not sell food.

Knowledge check 16

Give one reason why a business such as a luxury watch manufacturer may have a higher net profit margin than other watch manufacturers.

If the business was a retail clothing store then 10% net profit margin would be lower than the UK average of 12% in this market, meaning the business is not as effective at adding value and/or controlling its costs compared to the average. However, if the business was a retail electronics store, where the UK average is 6% net profit margin across the market, the business would be performing much better than competitors.

The benefit of using net profit margin is that the business can measure how efficient it is at keeping costs down and can use it to help determine effective pricing and cost reduction strategies. However, it does not indicate how many sales have been made and whether the pricing strategy adopted is realistic or not.

> **Exam tip**
>
> Pay careful attention to any figures you are given in an evaluation question. You need to be able to think about the type of business before giving any judgement.

Summary

After studying this topic, you should be able to:
- understand the role of the finance department and the purpose, benefits and drawbacks of different types of budget
- explain and evaluate the sources of internal and external finance including their use for a large business
- explain, construct and evaluate a cash-flow forecast and explain how it can help a business improve its performance
- explain the main components of an income statement and how a business might improve its profit, and complete calculations for gross and net profit
- calculate, interpret and evaluate gross and net profit margins

▉People in organisations (human resources)

The **human resource department's function** is to hire and train staff and keep records of their performance at work. It will ensure that the business abides by safety and employment regulations, such as holiday and sick leave entitlement, and assist managers in making decisions on staff performance and disciplinary issues.

Changes in working practices

Many jobs require staff to work full-time hours which are normally 42 hours per week. But there are other methods of working.
- **Multi-skilling** is the process of training employees to do several different jobs within the business, or to have a range of skills. Multi-skilling employees gives them the ability to cover many different roles and respond to rises and falls in demand. However, good training is essential if staff are to be efficient in their different roles.
- **Part-time staff** work shorter hours than full-time staff. Hours can be tailored to suit times of higher customer demand, such as in shops at weekends. However, it takes longer to train part-time staff.

Multi-skilling Training employees to do different jobs within the business, or to have a varied set of skills.

- **Temporary staff** are employed by the business for a specific period of time to cover periods of higher demand or staff absence. This helps the business to keep costs low. However, it will take time for the new members of staff to become productive.
- **Flexible hours** allow staff to vary the hours they work to meet the needs of the business and to some extent their own personal needs. The business can match the working hours of staff to periods of demand from customers. However, if staff are given too much flexibility in deciding their hours the business may not have sufficient staff to cope with customer demand.
- **Zero-hours contracts** are contracts where the business does not guarantee any work to the employee until demand means that they are needed. The business can match demand from customers with the employees' hours to meet that demand very precisely, reducing costs. However, employees may become demotivated if they feel undervalued by the company's refusal to guarantee them regular hours.
- **Homeworking** means that the employee does all or part of their job at home without the need to attend the businesses premises. This can allow the business to reduce the cost of providing workspace. However, staff may be less productive as the work is not supervised.
- **Job-sharing** allows two employees to share the responsibilities and benefits of a full-time member of staff. This allows the employer to keep the expertise and experience of valued employees, potentially motivating the staff. However, there are increased costs as there are two employees who need managing.
- **Hot-desking** is where desks in an office are not allocated to a specific member of staff but are allocated only when a member of staff needs to work at a desk. This means there are fewer costs from space being left empty due to staff absence. However, poor management of staff schedules can mean too many staff and not enough workspace.

The impact of new technology on working practices

The impact of new technology on working practices includes:

- Improved productivity and quality where machines can speed up manufacturing processes without making errors. Capacity utilisation also helps reduce the unit costs of each product.
- For employees, more flexible working practices and more emphasis on higher-level thinking skills can lead to improved staff recruitment, motivation and retention.
- However, many businesses have seen technology simply as a way to cut costs rather than a means of improving the worker experience.

Evaluating the impact of changing working patterns on employees and employers

These are some of the impacts of changes in working patterns on **employees**:

- More flexible working hours due to being able to work from home and attend meetings via the internet, rather than travelling large geographical distances.
- A move away from heavy industry to more service-sector roles.
- Manufacturing jobs made physically easier through the use of machinery.

Exam tip

Compare the benefits and drawbacks of different methods of staffing for a business.

- However, there has been a move to short-term contracts with little job security and low wages. This has become known as the 'gig economy'. Examples of gig economy employers are Uber and Deliveroo.
- The fact that staff are always 'switched on' to their jobs, for example through reading work-related messages at home, can cause stress and ultimately higher absenteeism and labour turnover.

These are some of the impacts of changes in working patterns on **employers**:

- Decreased costs as mechanisation has significantly reduced the numbers of manufacturing staff.
- Staff are more motivated, thanks to technology enabling more flexible working patterns.
- However, staff may have much less loyalty and be less productive if this flexibility is seen as only benefiting the employer's business, and not the staff themselves.

Workforce planning

Workforce planning means employing the correct number of staff with the right skills, in the right place and at the right time, to deliver the business's aims and objectives. Workforce planning includes establishing what vacancies exist, creating job descriptions and specifications, and advertising and training new members of staff to become a productive part of the business.

The benefits to a business of having effective workforce planning include:

- being more able to meet its objectives
- being able to respond to external factors more effectively
- gaining a competitive advantage

However, effective workforce planning can also includes the need for businesses to manage the reduction of staff, e.g. where heavy automation reduces the number of workers required.

Recruitment

Recruitment and selection is the process of finding and hiring the best-qualified candidate for a job, in a timely and cost-effective manner. Recruitment takes place through a **selection process**, the steps taken to advertise and choose the right employee for the vacancy.

Internal and external recruitment

The business can recruit new employees in two ways.

Internal recruitment means the business is looking to fill the job vacancy from within its existing workforce. This may give existing employees a chance of promotion. However, there may be fewer applications as recruitment is drawn from a smaller pool. Potentially, fewer employees in the business will have the right skills to apply.

External recruitment means the business is looking for external applicants for a vacancy. New employees are more likely to bring new ideas to the business and improve its competitive advantage. However, the process is more expensive and takes longer to complete than internal recruitment, as the job will be advertised in the media.

Recruitment and selection The process of finding and hiring the best-qualified candidate for a job.

Internal recruitment A job vacancy is filled from within a business's existing workforce.

External recruitment The business recruits an applicant from outside its existing workforce.

Exam tip

Compare the benefits and drawbacks of external and internal recruitment to a business.

Job analysis, job description and person specification

Recruitment and selection involves analysing the skills needed for the job (**job analysis**), issuing a **job description** with these skills and a profile of the type of person needed (**person specification**). The job is normally advertised and candidates are interviewed and selected based on who comes closest to meeting the description and specification.

The longer and more detailed the process, the costlier it is to the business. However, it is also more likely to be successful in securing the best employee for the job.

Evaluating appropriate methods of selecting employees for a job

There are various methods by which employees can be selected:

- **Interviews** are a chance for the employer to meet applicants and obtain information about their character, experience and suitability for the job. They are able to consider the candidate's suitability and their ability to respond well to questions in a pressured environment. The candidate has the chance to find out more about the job and how it would suit them. However, interviews are time consuming, and their effectiveness depends on the skills of the people conducting them.
- **Work trials** allow potential employees to spend some time working in the business so that the employer can assess their suitability for the job. A benefit is that it gives a realistic evaluation of applicants undertaking the actual role. However, applicants may not be tested realistically enough to make the process effective.
- **Testing** involves applicants completing a range of written tests to assess their qualities and skills, for example aptitude or personality tests. Testing can be useful in minimising the risk (and cost) to the business of recruiting the wrong candidate. However, they can create anxiety for candidates and possibly exclude some potentially good candidates, for example a person who has original ideas and can think creatively, but may not be the best performer in a test.
- **Selection exercises** are a range of activities that test candidates for key skills required for the job. This can include attending an assessment centre to undertake written tests together with teamworking and/or presentational activities. This gives the employer the chance to gather a greater level of detail on candidates, helping them to select the right person. But selection exercises can be expensive to design and administrate, making costs very high.
- **Telephone interviews** are similar to face-to-face interviews, with candidates being asked a set of questions to assess their suitability for the job. Telephone interviews may be used in the initial stage of the application process, to reduce the numbers of applicants invited to formal interviews. However, as the employer does not meet the applicants face-to-face, the interview may be less effective in establishing suitability for a job.

Evaluating the importance of recruitment to a business and its stakeholders

Recruitment is vitally important to a business and its stakeholders because an effective process can reduce the costs and problems associated with staff turnover.

Finding the right person for the job ensures that the business has the right set of skills to meet its objectives. Having a skilled and well-motivated workforce will help the business to achieve its objectives, enhancing productivity and the quality of the product delivery.

However, the recruitment process is time consuming and expensive, and less scientific than it might first appear.

Training

Training is the process whereby an individual acquires new skills and knowledge or improves their existing knowledge and skills base. The training of a new employee will often start with **induction training**, which introduces them to the business. **Job-specific training** will then be used to improve an individual's abilities to contribute to the business's needs.

On-the-job training is where employees are trained while carrying out an activity, often at their place of work. Types of on-the-job training include:

- **Demonstration** of the task or skill by someone who is proficient, i.e. showing the trainee how to do the job.
- **Coaching** from an expert member of staff, helping the employee learn and develop the skills required.
- **Job rotation**, where the employee is given different jobs in succession, so that they gain experience of a wide range of skills required in the business.

On-the-job training is cost effective for the business as the employee learns while working. However, the training may be reliant on the time another employee has available, which means it may not be as thorough as possible.

Off-the-job training is where employees are trained away from the job at a different location. For example, managers may attend leadership training courses, and student nurses spend some of their time at university attending lectures in addition to their on-the-job training in hospitals.

Off-the-job training can take place at an educational establishment such as a further education college, or for a specific period of time where the employee attends a course at a college or university for the entire working week, sometimes called block training.

Off-the-job training can offer a wider range of skills and/or qualifications than that based on the business's own field of expertise. However, external training can be expensive, involving travel costs as well as the cost of the course.

Apprenticeships are where a person agrees to work for a business to gain skills over a period of time, usually for lower rates of pay. Traditionally apprenticeships were found in trades such as plumbing, but increasingly they are also used in a wide range of professions such as the legal profession, where formal teaching and training in the workplace are combined to create a recognised qualification. Apprenticeships are a way for businesses to gain highly motivated staff for lower-level jobs. A problem is that they can often be misused as a way of gaining cheap labour, demotivating apprentices and leading to a poorer quality of output.

On-the-job training
Employees are trained through carrying out real tasks, usually in the workplace.

Off-the-job training
Training that happens outside the workplace.

Knowledge check 17

Why might a fast-food chain such as McDonald's not be able to simply train staff on the job?

Exam tip

Compare the benefits and drawbacks of on- and off-the-job training, and link this to theories of motivating employees.

Evaluating the importance and impact of training to a business and its stakeholders

Training is important because it ensures workers have the skills, experience and motivation to effectively help the business to achieve its aims and objectives.

- Induction training introduces new employees to the business, helping them understand its culture, structure, procedures and how they, as employees, fit in with meeting its objectives.
- Employees become productive and effective in the shortest time possible by learning the appropriate skills for their role.
- Good training will motivate staff, whose enhanced skills may lead on to greater responsibility, empowerment and earnings.
- However, training can be an expensive outlay for the business, disrupting production in the short term.

Appraisal

Appraisal is a system of reviewing the performance of workers. It usually takes the form of a discussion between the worker and the manager around pre-agreed objectives.

Methods of appraisal include:

- **Peer assessment**, where another employee will assess the performance of a colleague against agreed standards, highlighting areas done well and making constructive suggestions for improvement. Peer assessment can encourage empowerment and a team-based approach to improving performance. However, the person undertaking the assessment may not have the skills to carry out the task effectively, potentially creating difficulties and causing demotivation.
- **Self-assessment**, where the employee assesses their own performance, highlighting areas done well and those that need improvement. As with peer assessment, this can create a sense of empowerment and help to motivate staff, but the disadvantages are similar: some people find it difficult to be self-critical or balanced, leading to frustration and demotivation.
- **360-degree feedback**, a method of appraisal that gathers feedback from a number of people in the organisation, such as peers, managers and customers, in order to gain a fairer and more detailed view of the employee's performance against set objectives. An advantage is that all parties will feel it is a fair and balanced review, leading to greater trust and motivation to act on areas for improvement. The drawbacks are that the process is time consuming, and businesses may pay 'lip service' to the idea rather than engaging with it thoroughly, in which case employees may lose trust in the process and the outcomes.

Workforce performance

Workforce performance means the methods used by a business to assess their employees and their work processes to increase productivity and profitability.

Labour productivity is defined as the output per input of a person or machine per hour. It is a measure of the efficiency of a person or machine in converting inputs into useful outputs.

Appraisal A system used by a business to review the performance of individual members of staff.

Labour productivity A measure of the efficiency of a person or machine in converting inputs into useful outputs.

It is calculated as follows:

$$\textbf{labour productivity} = \frac{\text{output per time period}}{\text{number of employees at work}}$$

For example, if a business makes 5,000 products each hour and it takes 1,250 employee hours to produce this amount of product, labour productivity will be calculated as follows:

$$\text{labour productivity} = \frac{5,000}{1,250}$$

labour productivity = 4 units per employee hour

Labour productivity is a useful measure, as business efficiency and profitability are closely linked to the productive use of labour, and in order to remain competitive a business must keep its costs down.

Labour turnover is defined as the proportion of a firm's workforce that leaves during the course of a year. It is calculated as follows:

$$\textbf{labour turnover} = \frac{\text{staff leavers per year}}{\text{average number of staff}} \times 100$$

For example, if a firm has 10 people leave out of its staff of 100, the labour turnover would be:

$$\text{labour turnover} = \frac{10}{100} \times 100$$
$$= 10\%$$

Labour turnover can happen for many reasons, including retirement, illness and the business closing locations. Turnover varies depending on the industry, with turnover in retailing and hospitality typically being quite high. It also varies geographically: in areas with high unemployment, labour turnover is likely to be lower than the industry average, and vice versa.

Absenteeism is the proportion of employees not at work on a given day. The lower the absences, generally the more productive and efficient the business becomes. Some absences are planned for, such as holidays, but others are avoidable.

PriceWaterhouseCooper's report in January 2015 (*Absenteeism in the workplace*) states that the cost of sickness absences was £29 billion per year for UK businesses, with the average worker taking 9.1 days off sick compared to an average of 4.9 days in the USA.

Evaluating the importance of workforce performance for a business and its stakeholders

Internal factors that may affect labour turnover include poor recruitment and selection procedures and ineffective motivation or leadership, leading to low levels of worker commitment to the business. **External factors** include more alternative employment opportunities in the local area, and better transport links, allowing local workers to commute to other jobs.

The **negative effects** of high labour turnover include the costs of recruiting and training new staff, and a loss of productivity until new staff become efficient at their

Labour turnover The proportion of a firm's workforce that leaves during a year.

Absenteeism The proportion of employees absent from work on a given day.

job. **Positive effects** of labour turnover include new staff bringing an influx of fresh ideas and new skills to the business. Newly recruited staff may challenge existing procedures and methods that are inefficient or outdated, with a positive effect on productivity.

Organisational design

Organisational design is the process of aligning the structure of a business with its aims and objectives, in order to improve efficiency and effectiveness.

Authority is the power of a person to use and allocate resources in order to achieve business objectives. For example, for sole traders this will be the individual running the business.

Responsibility means the duty or obligation to perform and complete a task to the required standard. For example, a worker may have to complete a specific number of actions in a car production line per hour.

A hierarchy of a business is the order or levels of management from the highest to the lowest rank. The business hierarchy will show the chain of command, which is the line of authority from the top down to the bottom of the organisation.

A chain of command is the way the authority to take decisions is organised.

A span of control is the number of employees working directly under a manager.

The span of control can be described as either wide or narrow. A wide span of control (Figure 4) means that employees will have greater decision-making powers in the business, which may improve their levels of job satisfaction.

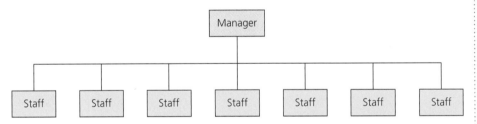

Figure 4 A wide span of control: one manager, many staff

A narrow span of control (Figure 5) means that employees will have fewer decision-making powers as there will be more managers supervising a smaller number of employees. Closer supervision should result in better control of employees' activities both individually and when working as a larger group.

Figure 5 A narrow span of control: one manager, few staff

Hierarchy of a business The levels of management from the highest to lowest rank.

Wide span of control Employees have greater decision-making powers in the business.

Narrow span of control Employees have less authority to make decisions, as there are more managers supervising them.

Knowledge check 18

Why might a business such as McDonald's operate a narrow span of control in its restaurants?

Exam tip

It can be useful to analyse the different types of organisational structure through Herzberg's two-factor theory. For example, a discussion of motivation through job enrichment evaluated against job security could help you to gain much higher marks.

Centralised and decentralised organisational structures

Centralisation means that decision-making is kept at the centre, not passed down to individual outlets/stores or individuals. Junior staff cannot complete tasks until managers give authority for them to do so.

Senior managers have more control over the business and can make standardised decisions that must be applied everywhere. This helps cost efficiency when the business benefits from the bulk purchase of raw materials. However, there may be too little flexibility to allow adjustments to variations in local tastes, and ambitious, creative junior staff may be driven to look for a job elsewhere.

Decentralisation means that a business gives the authority to make decisions to operating units such as stores or factories. Local managers are given plenty of scope to make decisions that may be quite bold and unexpected—Chicken McNuggets came from a franchisee's idea and was then adopted worldwide. However, the local decision-maker is only looking at a small part of the business and the business is less likely to benefit from cost savings of buying raw materials in bulk.

Tall, flat and matrix organisational structures

A **tall organisational structure** has many levels of hierarchy and the span of control is narrow. As there are many management layers, prospects of promotion are good. However, communication through the layers can take a long time, so the business may be less responsive in making the changes needed to remain competitive.

A **flat organisational structure** has few levels of hierarchy and a wide span of control. Communication takes a short amount of time so the business can be more responsive to changes needed to remain competitive. Employees can feel motivated as more decisions are **delegated** to them, so productivity may increase.

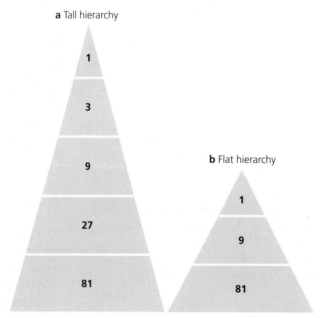

Figure 6 Organisational structures with the number of people at each level of the hierarchy

Exam tip

When evaluating centralisation or decentralisation, remember to relate this to motivational and leadership theories.

Tall organisational structure An organisational structure that has many levels of hierarchy and a narrow span of control.

Flat organisational structure An organisational structure with few levels of hierarchy and a wide span of control.

A **matrix organisational structure** is one in which individuals work across teams and projects as well as within their own department (see Table 7). For example, employees from the finance and human resources departments might work with designers and production staff on a new product for a customer.

A matrix structure can help to break down departmental barriers, improving communication across the entire organisation. However, members of project teams may have divided loyalties as they report to two managers.

Matrix organisational structure An organisational structure in which people can work across teams and projects as well as within their own department.

Table 7 Matrix organisational structure

	Marketing	Operations	Finance	Human Resources (HR)
	Marketing manager	*Operations manager*	*Finance manager*	*HR manager*
Project A (Team leader)	Marketing Team (A)	Operations Team (A)	Finance Team (A)	HR Team (A)
Project B (Team leader)	Marketing Team (B)	Operations Team (B)	Finance Team (B)	HR Team (B)
Project C (Team leader)	Marketing Team (C)	Operations Team (C)	Finance Team (C)	HR Team (C)
Project D (Team leader)	Marketing Team (D)	Operations Team (D)	Finance Team (D)	HR Team (D)

Delayering means that a business is removing one or more levels of hierarchy from its structure. This normally means that the span of control for managers will increase. A business might use delayering to cut costs and/or improve communications.

Delayering When a business removes one or more levels from its hierarchy.

The advantages and disadvantages of changing organisational structures and delayering

Advantages:

- Moving to a tall structure will allow a business to have greater control over the activities of staff lower down in the organisation, meaning they can control processes and quality more effectively.
- Delayering allows for more empowerment and better and quicker communication, leading to more motivated and productive staff.

Disadvantages:

- Not all organisations can run effectively with a flat or matrix structure, for example, those with staff who are low skilled and need more supervision.
- Matrix structures may be best suited to businesses in which staff spend most of their time working on projects. The risk is that staff have little accountability in situations where teams are formed and dispersed quickly.
- Delayering or moving to flat organisational structures can result in managers having excessive workloads and staff becoming less productive if they have not been well-enough trained to perform their wider roles.

Evaluating the choice between empowerment and control of the workforce

Empowerment allows employees the opportunity to undertake an increased number of tasks in a business. The tasks are those that give the employee more responsibility to make decisions and solve problems.

Exam tip

Look at the extract to spot which structure seems to be operated by the business, and question whether it is the most appropriate. Examiners credit students who can suggest a better approach for a business than that shown in the extract.

Empowerment When employees are given the authority, along with the skills, resources and opportunities, to undertake a wider variety of tasks or more demanding tasks.

The benefits of empowering the workforce can include:

■ faster problem-solving as employees who are closer to the problems have the chance to find solutions
■ increased motivation of staff which can improve productivity

The drawbacks of empowering the workforce can include:

■ staff being allowed to make decisions or undertake tasks for which they lack the necessary experience or training, increasing the risk of mistakes
■ a lack of co-coordination across the business if decision-making does not take into account the wider context of the business's activities, or decisions that are being made elsewhere in the company

Motivation

It is important for a business to motivate employees as this can lead to higher productivity, more creativity and ultimately greater profits. If a business fails to motivate its employees, it risks adverse consequences such as high staff turnover or lower productivity.

Motivational theories

F. W. Taylor (scientific management)

Taylor's theory of scientific management states that employees are mainly motivated by pay. Taylor also believed that employees need close supervision and should only carry out small tasks they can repeat to become efficient. Workers should be paid a **piece rate**, an amount paid for each task done, motivating them to do as many as possible.

A benefit of Taylor's theory is that workers are encouraged to increase productivity. However, Taylor employees are likely to be demotivated by boring jobs, leading to high labour turnover.

Piece rate An amount paid for each completed task.

Mayo

Mayo believed that employees are motivated by social needs (something that Taylor ignored), known as the **human relations theory** of motivation, which encourages managers to take a greater interest in workers. A benefit of Mayo's theory should be that, through valuing staff opinions and encouraging teamwork, a business has a more motivated workforce, resulting in better productivity. However, staff don't always have the same objectives as the business, and communication between employees and managers is not always positive, which could result in low productivity gains.

Maslow's hierarchy of needs

Maslow's theory of motivation is that there are five levels of human needs which employees need to have fulfilled at work, structured into a **hierarchy**, as shown in Figure 7. Only once lower-level needs have been met do the higher needs start to matter.

In encouraging the business to create an environment for employees that satisfies these different needs, Maslow's theory should help it to motivate staff, leading to higher productivity. But many critics suggest that esteem needs and self-actualisation can never be achieved in some lower-skilled roles, such as street sweepers or toilet attendants.

Figure 7 Maslow's hierarchy of needs

Herzberg's two-factor theory

Herzberg's theory of motivation states that certain factors (**motivators**) cause job satisfaction which encourages employees to work harder, such as responsibility and recognition for achievement. A separate set of factors (**hygiene factors**) cause job dissatisfaction. Herzberg believed pay was not a motivator, but only a source of job dissatisfaction, if pay was too low. In this case staff could go on strike or become hostile in the workplace.

Knowledge check 19

Name one benefit to Google of using Maslow's theory of motivation for those employees designing new products.

Herzberg's motivators – these **satisfiers** relate to the job itself and can create positive motivation

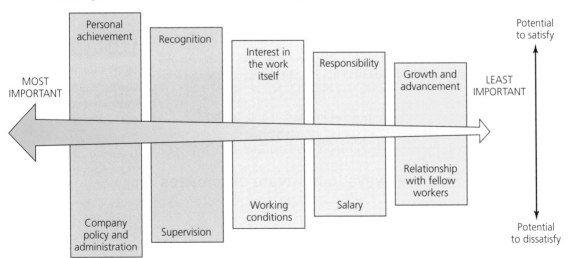

Herzberg's hygiene factors – these relate to the job environment and have the potential to dissatisfy

Figure 8 Herzberg's hygiene and motivational factors

According to Herzberg's theory, focusing on meaningful tasks would promote higher levels of motivation and productivity. However, this presumes there is a link between job satisfaction and productivity, an assumption which has since been questioned.

Vroom's expectancy theory

Victor H. Vroom's expectancy theory states that an employee's motivation is an outcome of how much an individual wants a reward. The theory is based on the view that employees consciously decide how well to perform a job, based on the effort–performance relationship, which is the likelihood that the individual's efforts will be recognised by the business. It is also based on the performance–reward relationship, which is the extent to which the employee believes a good performance will lead to rewards. Vroom also believed there was a rewards–personal goals relationship, which is about the attractiveness of the potential rewards to the individual. To motivate staff, businesses should ensure jobs are interesting and challenging and that performance is rewarded.

Porter and Lawler's expectancy theory

Porter and Lawler's expectancy theory expanded Vroom's theory by categorising a reward as either **intrinsic**, meaning the positive feelings an individual might experience on completing a task well, or **extrinsic**, meaning a reward that comes from outside the individual, such as a bonus. Porter and Lawler also stated that motivation is affected by an individual's ability to perform a task and their perception of it.

A strength of expectancy theory is that it is based on the self-interest of the worker, who will want to achieve the maximum satisfaction and minimum dissatisfaction in terms of receiving or not receiving rewards. However, the theory ignores the reality that many businesses offer rewards that are not linked only to performance, but may depend on the individual's position in the business or their educational attainment.

Evaluating motivational theories and their importance to businesses

Motivational theories are important to businesses as they give managers a set of tools to help increase quality, productivity and the efficiency of staff through financial and non-financial methods.

However, the theories do not provide any guidance as to when, if and in what circumstances they should be used, and the success of any attempt to use them will be influenced by factors such as the employees' own personal motivations.

Financial and non-financial ways to motivate employees

Financial incentives to improve employee performance include:
- **Piecework.**
- **Commission**, where a payment is made as a percentage of the value of the good or service sold.
- **Bonuses**, extra payments made to recognise an employee's contribution to a business.
- **Profit share**, where the more profit the business makes, the greater share of this the worker receives.

> **Exam tip**
>
> Motivational theories can be used in many evaluative questions, particularly where there is a focus on reducing costs or improving quality. Remember, staff often provide the creative driving force behind a business, so costs and quality are likely to suffer if the business forgets that motivating staff is key to achieving its objectives.

- **Performance-related pay**, a business's attempt to link pay to increased productivity by the employee.
- **Share ownership**, where employees have the opportunity to receive shares in the business they work for, either free or at a discounted price. This is often used to motivate employees and particularly managers to achieve targets. For example, John Lewis's staff own all the shares in the business.

Taylor's theory of motivating employees is based on financial incentives. Maslow's theory regards pay as a basic need, while Herzberg treats it as a hygiene factor.

Non-financial techniques to improve employee performance include:
- **Delegation**, where managers give responsibility for a task to an employee.
- **Consultation**, where employees will be asked for their views on business-related issues, although managers may not act on them.
- **Empowerment**, where official authority is given to employees to make decisions and control their own activities.
- **Teamworking**, where employees work in small groups with a common aim.
- **Flexible working**, which is a way of working that suits an employee's needs.
- **Job enrichment**, where employees are given greater responsibility and recognition by extending their role in the production process.
- **Job rotation**, where jobs or tasks are changed from time to time to reduce boredom and provide greater labour flexibility.
- **Job enlargement**, where an employee will be given additional work which is similar to their current role.

Non-financial incentives can be linked to all of the theories of employee motivation except for Taylor's. For Maslow, they tend to satisfy the higher-level needs. Herzberg suggested job enrichment as the key to human motivation.

Evaluating the appropriateness of financial and non-financial methods of motivation to a business and its stakeholders

The appropriateness of the different methods of motivation will depend on:
- How much they will cost. For example, a business that is struggling to make a profit may feel that investment in employee motivation is not appropriate, as survival is its most important issue. However, the very reason for poor performance may be a lack of such motivators.
- The nature of the business.
- The nature of the employees. For example, highly skilled workers may value non-financial incentives.
- The ethical position of the business, including its shareholders and wider stakeholders.

Evaluating the impact of a motivated workforce on a business and its stakeholders

A motivated workforce is generally seen as a positive asset for any business as it reduces costs. Highly motivated staff generally need less supervision, provide better customer service and produce higher-quality products.

Knowledge check 20

How could profit sharing be used at the supermarket Morrison's to improve the overall profits of the business?

Knowledge check 21

How can job rotation on the BMW Mini production line help the business improve the quality of its products?

Exam tip

Always start an exam answer on motivation with an academic definition, such as Herzberg's who defined motivation as 'doing something because you want to do it'.

However, businesses should not underestimate the importance of getting other key elements of its offering right, such as a good product at the right price. Otherwise the most motivated workforce in the world will not be able to achieve the key objectives of the business, such as making a profit.

Management and leadership

Management means the creating, controlling and directing of the business's resources in order to achieve its objectives. The functions and roles of management include planning, leading, organising and controlling all aspects of the business including its workforce, raw materials and production facilities.

Management by objectives

Management by objectives means improving the business performance through clearly defined objectives for managers and employees. Objectives need to be SMART:

- **Specific:** that is, they should meet the specific needs and wants of customers and the organisation.
- **Measurable:** so that anyone can see whether they have been achieved.
- **Achievable:** challenging but not impossible.
- **Relevant:** to the needs of the business and its stakeholders.
- **Timely:** have a specific time scale attached to them.

The benefits of management by objectives include:

- clear objectives, allowing for the measurement of performance and improvement at all levels of the organisation
- a clear idea of the priorities that managers should have, the standard they need to achieve and the deadline for doing so

The drawbacks of management by objectives include :

- the organisation will need to invest significant time and money for the process to be effective
- objectives are often set that are not SMART, leading to demotivated staff, poor productivity and business failure

McGregor's theory X and theory Y

McGregor's theory X and theory Y outline two styles of management. Theory X managers take a pessimistic view of workers, believing they are motivated by rewards and punishments and generally dislike work and avoid responsibility. Appraisals are often looking for quantifiable results such as increased sales or output, which are used to control staff.

Theory Y managers have a positive view of workers and use a participation style of management. They are trust-based, encourage collaboration and support the idea that workers should take on more responsibility and develop their skills. They presume that workers are happy to work on their own initiative, that they are self-motivated and want to be involved in decision-making.

Leadership styles

The difference between management and leadership is that it is the manager's job to plan, organise and coordinate. The leader's job is to set clear goals, then help managers see how to achieve them.

Leadership may inspire creativity and risk-taking in a way management does not. It can fall into the following types:

■ **Autocratic**: an autocratic leader makes all the decisions independently of employees and shares Taylor's attitude to staff. Communication tends to be top-down, with little delegation. Decision-making is quickly put into practice throughout the business with no consultation with employees. As a result, employees can feel undervalued as they have no say in how decisions are made, leading to demotivation and loss of productivity.

■ **Paternalistic**: more account is taken of the needs and views of workers. The leader is interested in workers' wellbeing and acts as a paternal (or parental) figure, consulting employees and listening to their feedback or opinions, although still making the final decisions. This style is closely linked with Mayo and Maslow's views of motivation. Employees feel more motivated as they believe their views are recognised and understand why decisions are made, leading to improved productivity. However, there is little delegation, and opportunities for employees to influence decisions are limited.

■ **Democratic**: the leader encourages others to participate in decision-making through consultation, often acting on the majority opinion on an issue, and often favouring delegation. This style is linked to Herzberg's theory on motivation. An advantage is that employees will be more likely to be committed to decisions they have been involved in making. The drawback is that consultation-based decisions tend to take a long time to make, meaning the business is not as responsive to change.

■ **Laissez-faire**: indecision or absence at the top creates a decision-making vacuum which is filled by more junior staff, with employees able to be resourceful and creative. A benefit is that innovation and empowerment could lead to a more competitive business. But there may be little incentive for employees to work hard and lines of communication can be confused, leading to lower productivity.

■ **Bureaucratic**: based on fixed duties in a hierarchy of authority, where the leader applies a set of rules to make decisions. It is often used in businesses that require little creativity from employees. The advantage of bureaucratic leadership is that a business can easily recreate such leadership across its network and efficiently manage staff who do repetitive tasks. Its weakness is that the approach can stifle managers and staff who are innovative and can lead to demotivation and poor levels of productivity.

Leadership theories

Theories of leadership include:

■ **F. Fielder's contingency theory** which proposed that the quality of leadership was the most important factor affecting the success of a business. Leaders should have traits such as being friendly and supportive rather than being hostile and uncooperative. Leadership should also reflect the situation — 'contingency' — that the leader finds themselves in, and they should mould their style to meet the situation. Relationship-orientated leaders were judged to be effective in less extreme circumstances, whereas task-orientated leaders were better in extremely difficult or extremely favourable situations.

Autocratic leadership
The leader makes all the decisions independently of employees.

Paternalistic leadership
More attention is given to the needs and views of workers. Employees are consulted for their ideas, although the leader ultimately makes the decisions.

Democratic leadership
The leader encourages others to participate in decision-making through consultation and delegation.

Bureaucratic leadership
A leadership style that makes use of a hierarchy of authority in which decisions are based on the application of rules.

Knowledge check 22

Name a difference between autocratic and laissez-faire styles of leadership.

■ **P. Wright and D. Taylor's theory** which suggested that it was possible to improve a leader's abilities through education. They identified skills that leaders needed such as verbal and non-verbal skills, and a checklist to diagnose what was required in a specific work situation. A leader's ability to adapt to the situation would improve worker performance. Wright and Taylor believed that regardless of a manager's leadership style, staff would perform better with leaders who had excellent interpersonal skills.

Employer–employee relationships

Employer–employee relations means the individual and collective relationship the employer has with employees in the workplace. Good employer–employee relations help create high levels of employee involvement and commitment in achieving the objectives of the business.

This can include the duties and rights of employers and employees such as:

■ **A contract of employment**, which is an oral or written agreement between employer and employee stating the duties, terms and conditions of employment in return for payment.
■ **Health and safety**, where the employer and employee have legal obligations to ensure the workplace and the methods used to undertake the work are safe, for example wearing protective clothing.
■ **The minimum wage**, which is the lowest hourly rate of pay that employers are obliged to pay. For example, in 2017 the minimum wage for under-18s was £4.05 per hour.
■ **The living wage**, which is the minimum hourly pay rate for employees aged 25 or over. This was £7.50 in 2017.
■ **Dismissal**, when an employer makes someone leave their job due to dissatisfaction with their performance.

Equal opportunities

Equal opportunities means the right to be treated without discrimination. A focus on equal opportunities emphasises opportunities for education, employment and advancement within a business. The **Equality Act 2010** is the law that protects people from discrimination in the workplace, for example discrimination based on race, sex or disability.

The benefits of equal opportunities include:

■ Awarding jobs on employees' merits alone means the business has access to levels of skills and experience that will most likely give it a competitive advantage against its rivals.
■ Most stakeholders, including customers, are likely to see equal opportunities as a positive feature of a business and its products, which may encourage them to choose its products over those of less ethical competitors.

The drawbacks of equal opportunities include:

■ In the short-term, the costs of conducting interviews and the training and development of staff may increase.
■ There is a risk that businesses have an unbalanced view of what equal opportunities actually means, leading to accusations of political correctness and bad PR.

Exam tip

Leadership often links to motivational theories in an evaluation question. You need to look at a range of issues including the business's structure and then make a judgement as to how the leadership style affects the business. For example, the autocratic approach could be best if the business needs quick decisions.

Employer–employee relations The individual and collective relationship the employer has with employees in the workplace.

Exam tip

A question on redundancy will normally need a discussion about employees as a cost to the business.

Trade unions

A **trade union** is an association of workers in a trade or a profession, which protects and enhances the rights of its members, for example by negotiating pay and even redundancy packages.

Collective bargaining is where a business negotiates with representatives of employees, such as trade unions, regarding the terms and conditions of employment. The negotiations will be about gaining similar benefits for all employees.

Collective bargaining allows the business to potentially save time and money by negotiating with a small number of representatives from a trade union. It usually gives employees more bargaining power. However, it may lessen the benefits for more experienced staff as the union will be keen to ensure all members, including junior staff, receive similar benefits, rather than arguing for different pay and terms of employment for those with greater skills and experience.

A **trade dispute** is where workers and the employer are arguing or negotiating over conditions of employment. For example, in 2017 the National Union of Rail, Maritime and Transport Workers (RMT) was taking part in a long-running dispute over their employer's decision to run trains with only a driver and no conductor.

Industrial action is where employees, usually in the form of a trade union, protest over some element of working conditions. This can include withdrawing their labour for a period of time — going on strike — or working to rule, which means employees will only do what they are contractually obliged to do.

The employer and the union/workers can attempt **dispute resolution** through:

- **Negotiation**, where a discussion between the union/workers and the employer takes place to reach an agreement.
- **Consultation**, where the union/workers are asked for ideas and input on an issue before the employer makes a decision.
- **Arbitration**, where the disputing parties may be helped by the **Advisory, Conciliation and Arbitration Service (ACAS)**, a government organisation with expertise in industrial relations. ACAS can provide specialists to listen to each party's grievances and suggest solutions. ACAS cannot impose a solution on the parties.

Evaluating the impact of employer–employee relations on the business and its stakeholders

- Good relations mean a smooth-running business along the lines of a partnership between staff and employers.
- Staff who feel they are part of the decision-making process are more likely to accept even difficult decisions such as redundancies.
- Ultimately good relations lead to lower costs, a more flexible and dynamic business and higher profits.
- However, a lack of involvement and employees or employers with their own agenda can be counterproductive and cause disputes, leading to strikes, lower productivity and ultimately business failure.

Trade union An association of workers in a trade or a profession, formed to defend and advance their rights and interests.

Collective bargaining Representatives of employees, such as trade unions, negotiate with employers regarding the terms and conditions of employment.

Summary

After studying this topic, you should be able to:

- understand the role of the human resources department and the changes in different working patterns for the workforce
- evaluate the impact of new technology on the working patterns of the workforce and on the business
- explain and evaluate workforce planning, training and appraisal, and their importance to the business
- explain and calculate labour productivity, labour turnover, labour retention and absenteeism and evaluate the importance of workforce performance to the success of the business
- explain and evaluate organisational design, empowerment and motivational theories such as those by Taylor, Mayo and Maslow
- explain the financial and non-financial methods of motivating employees, management by objectives and leadership styles and their importance to business success
- explain and evaluate equal opportunities, trade unions, workplace conflict and methods of resolution

Operations management

Operations management means the methods used by the business to create products and services that are efficiently delivered to the customer to maximise profits and reduce costs.

For example, the car manufacturer Tesla is in the process of creating the world's biggest battery production facility for its electric cars. In order to keep costs low the factory is located next to the facility that creates the cars, is highly automated with robots and has the ability to produce the batteries on a massive scale.

On a much smaller scale, Heck Sausages is a family-run, niche producer of sausages which values the uniqueness and handmade quality of its meat products, so it has a production line that works in batches. This is to ensure that the highest quality is maintained and that product lines can be tweaked for different customer requirements.

Added value

Added value means enhancing the gap between the production cost and the selling price. Customers may perceive the product as better than competitor products for a number of reasons, including the brand image or the business image enhancing brand loyalty. For example, VW Group is responsible for building a number of brands of car including Skoda and Audi. The engines used in the production of Skodas are the same as the engines used in Audis, allowing the VW Group to cut its costs of raw materials by buying in bulk, one method of adding value. VW Group have also built on the brand image of Audi to, allowing it to sell Audi cars at a premium price compared to Skodas, another method of adding value.

To calculate added value the formula is:

added value = selling price of product − cost of production

For example, the Sony PlayStation 4 cost £295 to manufacture when it was released in November 2013. It was sold for £349 to retail customers. The added value was therefore:

added value = £349 – £295

added value = £54

To increase added value a business can:

- **build a brand** which has a reputation for quality for which customers will pay a premium price
- **add features** to the product which differentiate it from others in the market
- **offer convenience** such as being able to buy a book from WH Smith at the train station at a premium price
- **provide outstanding customer service**, as you would expect if you paid £50 for the afternoon tea experience at Claridge's Hotel, rather than paying a lower price somewhere less well known

The benefits of added value to a business include:

- being able to charge higher prices, and therefore make a greater profit
- acting as a unique selling point, differentiating a product from a competitor's

The drawbacks of added value include:

- higher prices create high expectations which the business may not be able to achieve, resulting in customer dissatisfaction and lost sales
- a significant amount of investment and time is needed to create added value, so a business must have the funds to enable this

Production

Production is defined as the total amount of output produced in a specific time period. The more that can be produced in a specific period of time, the more efficient the business becomes in using its resources.

Methods of production

There are a number of ways a business can produce its products:

- **Job production**, where a business concentrates on producing a single unit at a time, then starting the next one. This enables products to be tailor-made to the needs of the customer and is suited to niche-market products. A single worker or group of workers complete the task, often with high levels of skill. The advantages of job production are that it usually produces a high-quality product that meets the needs of the individual customer, and that there is greater job satisfaction for employees. A problem is that production costs are likely to be high.
- **Batch production**, involving the manufacture of a number of goods (the batch) at the same time. One stage of the manufacturing process must be completed for the whole batch before the products move on to the next stage of the process. Making products in batches reduces the unit costs. Specific customer needs can still be met and specialist machinery or skills can increase the number produced in a specific period of time. Problems include lower productivity due to time lost switching between different batches.

Exam tip

When evaluating added value try to look at the wider picture of the business and its market. High-value brands such as Apple find it much easier to promote added value and the premium prices that go with it than little-known businesses.

Knowledge check 23

Give one reason why Tesla producing its own batteries for its electric cars adds more value than buying them from another business.

Production The total amount of output produced in a specific time period.

Job production A method of production in which a business concentrates on producing a single unit at a time.

Batch production Manufacturing a number of goods at the same time.

■ **Flow production** is organised so that units move directly from one operation to the next in a continuous sequence. This method relies on having large demand for a standardised product, usually a mass-market product. Flow production uses a large proportion of machines compared to staff so that many products can be made at a relatively low cost. There is the additional advantage of being able to buy raw materials in bulk and at a lower unit cost. Disadvantages include large initial capital costs for the amount of machinery needed, and the fact that it can be time consuming and expensive to make any changes to the production process.

Flow production A method of production in which units move directly from one operation to the next in a continuous sequence.

Exam tip

An exam question may ask you to compare two types of production and recommend the most suitable. The key to high marks is to look carefully at the market the business is in. For example, is it selling to a niche or a mass market?

Knowledge check 24

Give one reason why a supplier of clothing to Primark might choose flow production.

Productivity

Productivity is defined as the output per input of a person or machine per hour. Productivity is therefore a measure of the efficiency of a person or machine in converting inputs into useful outputs.

The more productive a business is, the better it can compete with others in the same market. This is because higher productivity can be passed on to customers in terms of lower prices which may give the business a competitive advantage and increased market share.

A business can try to improve its productivity by:
■ **Training employees**, which will help them learn more effective ways of completing their tasks. However, training costs money.
■ **Improving motivation** using different leadership styles and financial and non-financial incentives. But there are costs associated with creating incentives and some methods can be counterproductive and demotivate some employees, such as piecework.
■ **Buying more or better capital equipment**, which can increase productivity or actually replace employees in the task of production completely. The drawback is that machinery is expensive and may not offer the flexibility to change the production process in the way that staff can.
■ **Buying better quality raw materials**, which can reduce the time wasted on rejected products. However, costs are likely to rise which may offset the productivity savings.

Knowledge check 25

Give one reason why a business may decide to aim for lower productivity.

Exam tip

Productivity can be applied not only to making products but also selling them or even delivering a service. When evaluating productivity try to think of the trade-offs and opportunity cost issues related to improving it.

Capacity utilisation

Capacity utilisation measures the proportion of current output compared with the maximum possible output in a given time period. It can be shown as a percentage using the following formula:

$$\text{capacity utilisation} = \frac{\text{actual output}}{\text{maximum possible output}} \times 100$$

Capacity utilisation Measures the proportion of current output compared with the maximum possible output.

For example, where a business has the potential to make 4,000 pairs of headphones per day, but the actual output of headphones on a particular day is 3,200 the capacity utilisation is as follows:

$$\text{capacity utilisation} = \frac{3,200}{4,000} \times 100$$

capacity utilisation = 80%

The figure gives a measure of productive efficiency and the higher the percentage, the lower the unit costs. With high capacity utilisation, the business is using its assets effectively, making the business more competitive, which should lead to higher profits. A business may have a low capacity utilisation for a number of reasons such as low demand, inefficient production, or because the introduction of new technology to increase capacity has not yet been matched by increased demand.

When a business is operating at less than 100% capacity there is said to be **spare capacity**.

An example of how fixed costs relates to capacity is shown in Table 8.

Table 8 Fixed costs and capacity of a football stadium

	Full stadium	Half-empty stadium
	50,000 fans	25,000 fans
Weekly salary bill (fixed costs)	£750,000	£750,000
Salary fixed cost per fan	£15 (750,000/50,000)	£30 (750,000/25,000)

Here, when the football stadium is only half full, capacity utilisation is 50%. This means that the weekly salary bills are split over only 25,000 fans and £30 of the ticket price is needed to pay for wages. When the capacity utilisation is 100% with 50,000 fans, then the fixed costs are only £15 of the ticket price.

Ways of improving capacity utilisation

Capacity utilisation can be improved by:
- Increasing workforce hours by introducing extra shifts or employing temporary staff.
- Improving marketing, which can lead to higher demand for the products.
- Cutting the capacity of the factory, for example by buying smaller premises. This will reduce fixed costs and the costs per unit, helping the business remain competitive.

The benefits of using capacity utilisation as a measure include:
- It can indicate how efficient a business is in producing its products. The closer to 100%, the better.
- As utilisation becomes higher, the average costs of producing each product fall, allowing the business to be more competitive.

The problems of using capacity utilisation as a measure include:
- The higher the utilisation, the greater the difficulty in producing a product with consistent quality, particularly where production is labour rather than capital-intensive.
- High utilisation can put pressure on the workforce who may become stressed and demotivated, causing higher levels of absenteeism.

Knowledge check 26

How could a supermarket increase capacity utilisation if demand is low?

Exam tip

A more sophisticated evaluation of a business's capacity utilisation could conclude that the benefits of some under-utilisation outweigh the costs. You need to look at the type of business and market to consider what is appropriate.

Knowledge check 27

Why might a business with a large workforce find it extremely difficult to achieve 100% capacity?

Technology

Technology is the use of machinery, devices and scientific knowledge to create and sell a product or service.

- **Information technology** is important to a business because it can produce cost savings, better quality products and lower unit costs. However, to achieve a competitive advantage a significant investment in unique technology is required.
- **Computer-aided design (CAD)** is a method of producing accurate designs and drawings of products in 2D or 3D using computer programs. The vast majority of mass-produced products start life on a computer. The strengths of CAD are the ability to draw a product to scale and to amend and manipulate the design to meet the needs and wants of the end user, so saving time and money. A drawback is that CAD packages are expensive to purchase and require highly skilled staff to operate them.
- **Computer-aided manufacture (CAM)** is technology that uses software to run machinery such as robots in order to create products on a production line. CAD can be linked to CAM to form an end-to-end automated production process. A benefit of CAM is that it offers higher speed, greater accuracy and greater consistency in quality, running 24 hours a day. But set-up costs are high and unit costs can be high for low-volume production.
- **Robotics** is the use of programmable machines to design and construct complex products from raw materials. An advantage is that they can perform many tasks quickly and precisely, with less waste leading to lower unit costs. The disadvantages are that they require a huge initial investment, regular maintenance and a significant amount of programming for every change made to a product.

Lean production

Lean production is a philosophy which aims to minimise costs and enhance quality by using a range of waste-saving measures. Anything that does not add value to the production process, such as buffer stock, repairs of faulty products and unnecessary movements of staff and the product around the business, is reduced.

Lean production aims for **continuous improvement**. Businesses using lean production will ask employees to identify any areas of the production process that can be improved. If waste can be avoided, costs will be reduced and a competitive advantage will be obtained in the market.

A range of techniques are used to reduce waste and improve productivity, including:

- **Kaizen** (a Japanese word meaning 'change for the better') is aimed at fostering continuous improvement. Small groups of workers from an area of a firm meet together regularly to discuss ways of improving quality (and other aspects of efficiency). The benefits of Kaizen include increased productivity due to reduced waste in the production process, which in turn reduces costs. However, staff may not wish to be involved in the process, and setting it up incurs extra costs.

Lean production An approach which aims to minimise costs by cutting out wasteful practices while maintaining high quality.

Knowledge check 28

How might a business using lean production encourage its workers to minimise costs?

Exam tip

Try to judge the feasibility of businesses being able to successfully use JIT stock control and lean production. Often a business is either too small or lacks the close relationship with suppliers needed to make this process work instead of traditional stock control. Look at the situation carefully before recommending this approach.

Kaizen Practices to promote continuous improvement, such as asking groups of workers to share ideas about working more efficiently.

- **Just-in-time** (JIT) management of stock means that inputs into the production process arrive only when they are needed. Just-in-time production is not driven by supply but aims to meet customer demand exactly in time, quality and quantity. The aim is to improve the overall competitiveness of the business by holding no buffer stock and relying on deliveries of raw materials and components to arrive exactly when they are needed, going straight to the factory floor. JIT is what is known as a **'pull' system** of production, where orders for products act as the mechanism for the business to produce them. It requires careful planning, with a large investment in computer software which links each sale to suppliers' production software. The benefits of JIT include lower stock holding, meaning less storage space is required, rent and insurance costs are lower and less working capital is tied up in stock. But there are disadvantages. Mistakes in the production process can mean a failure to meet customer orders, the process is heavily reliant on having excellent relations with suppliers to ensure deliveries are made on time, and the business may not enjoy the benefits of buying materials in bulk.

> **Just-in-time** A stock management strategy which aims to increase efficiency by receiving raw materials only when they are needed in the production process.

- **Cell production** is where the production line is organised into small teams (cells) with each cell having its own responsibility for a part of the finished product. Each cell acts in turn as a supplier, feeding the next cell in the production line, and as a customer from cells further back down the chain. Staff in each cell can complete many jobs in the production of the product, so cell production allows for job rotation. The cell is also responsible for completing work, covering absences and identifying recruitment and training needs, thus allowing for job enrichment. Cell production has various strengths. For example, working in teams can improve communication, and multi-skilling can motivate staff and create more flexibility to meet the business's future needs. A drawback can be that staff may feel demotivated if they are constantly pushed for more and more output and improvements, leading to absenteeism.

> **Cell production** A system in which the production line consists of small teams (cells), with each cell responsible for a significant part of the end product.

- **Time-based management** is an approach that seeks to reduce the level of wasted time in a production process. A benefit of using time-based management is that it reduces lead times and allows for a quicker response to customer needs. But a business may not be able to benefit from economies of scale as it will only order sufficient materials to meet current customer needs.

The benefits of lean production include:

- A decrease in waste in terms both of worker time and raw materials, saving costs.
- As workers are encouraged to work in teams and look for improvements, this leads to more empowerment, increased motivation and productivity.

The drawbacks of lean production include:

- Businesses potentially struggling to meet orders if their suppliers cannot deliver raw materials on time.
- The economies of scale from bulk buying may not be available due to the emphasis on waste reduction, leading to higher unit costs.

Quality

Quality means the features of a product or service that allow it to satisfy customer needs. Quality is an important factor in gaining competitive advantage for a business: if customers are consistently satisfied with a product or service, it will increase their loyalty to the brand, and therefore the company's market share and profit.

Customers who value quality will often pay a premium price for a product over other similar products. Quality can therefore act as a unique selling point.

Quality is an important aim for just-in-time and lean production, particularly as waste includes products that do not meet customer needs. There are different ways of controlling quality:

- **Quality control** is the process of inspecting products to ensure that they meet the required quality standard. Unsatisfactory products are filtered out before they reach the customer, at the end of the production process. As specially trained employees perform quality control, any defects in products are more likely to be spotted before the goods reach the customer. However, there may be problems if all staff are not encouraged to take responsibility for the quality of the product. Also, quality control by itself does not eliminate waste but only ensures the customer gains the right quality of product.

- **Quality assurance** aims to design systems in which mistakes are less likely, with the emphasis on establishing a set of procedures and standards that all workers must follow. The aim is to have zero defects with staff encouraged to do more checking of their own work. Benefits include lower costs, as the checking procedures mean less wastage and less time spent reworking products. However, the risk is that staff see the checking of their own work as simply a 'tick box' exercise with no real value, in which case it may not be done effectively.

- **Total quality management (TQM)** is a philosophy of getting all workers to take responsibility for building better quality into their own jobs, striving to get things right the first time and every time. To achieve TQM, the following approaches can be employed by a business:
  - Encouraging strong **teamwork** such as the open sharing of information about problems that have occurred and their causes.
  - Each team, called a **quality chain**, treats another person or team as a customer and aims to get the quality right first time.
  - **Empowerment** allows each individual in a team to have greater control over how they organise and complete tasks with the business setting overall targets.
  - **Monitoring**, where the current performance of each team is assessed against established targets.
  - **Zero defects**, where teams and individuals are motivated to prevent mistakes by developing a desire to do their job right the first time.
  - **Quality circles**, groups of employees who do similar work, which meet together regularly to analyse problems and suggest ways product quality can be improved.

The advantages of TQM are that faults and problems are spotted and resolved quickly. Teamwork and extra responsibility can raise the motivation levels of staff which can also increase quality and productivity. However, the introduction of TQM, which

Quality control The process of inspecting products to ensure that they meet the required quality standards.

Quality assurance A process which aims to reduce the risk of mistakes by ensuring that workers adhere to a set of procedures and standards.

Total quality management (TQM) An approach in which all workers are meant to take responsibility for improving the quality of their work.

Quality circles Groups of employees who meet regularly to identify potential improvements in quality.

will involve training staff and ensuring the production process is flexible enough to adapt to the new systems, will take time and money with benefits not being seen for some time.

- **Benchmarking** is a process in which businesses look at comparable organisations, normally with better performance in a particular area, to see what lessons can be learned to improve their own performance. Benefits include highlighting areas of improvement in quality, productivity and costs, allowing the business to become more competitive. The problem is that undertaking benchmarking with competitors is actually very difficult, as they are unlikely to want to give away the secrets of their success, and the activity tends to focus on narrow processes rather than other factors that lead to business success.

Purchasing

Purchasing means the acquisition of raw materials or products by a business.

Suppliers are important in this process as they are responsible for ensuring the raw materials/products are delivered in sufficient quantity at the right time and to the right level of quality. Working in partnership with suppliers is key to a business's ultimate success.

Stock is the value of the products kept on the business premises at any one time. Stock can be raw materials, work-in-progress or stocks of finished goods awaiting a customer. **Stock control** is the attempt by businesses to ensure that stock levels are managed efficiently. There is a balance between holding enough stock to meet demand and not holding too much, so as to save on stock-holding costs.

> **Stock control** How businesses try to ensure that stock levels are managed efficiently.

Methods of stock control

The more efficient the business becomes at managing stock levels, the less money is tied up in current assets and the better the working capital is at any one time.

- **Just-in-case stock control** means the business keeps a certain amount of stock in reserve to allow for problems such as late delivery by suppliers or unexpected demand.
- **Just-in-time (JIT) management of stock** is where the raw materials needed for the production process arrive only when they are needed. JIT aims to reduce spending on stock and improve the overall competitiveness of the business by eliminating the costs of unnecessarily high stock levels. Instead of large deliveries to a warehouse, materials arrive just when they are needed and are taken straight to the factory floor.
- **Computerised stock control** can be used for either just-in-case or JIT, and is the process of checking stocks using a computer system, which will reorder any items that have been identified as required. Think of a supermarket self-service checkout where you scan in the barcode. With just-in-case, stock will be delivered to a stock room to ensure there are always reserves available. With JIT, stock will only be delivered at the point the software has decided a delivery is required to meet the immediate demand.

Interpretation of stock-control diagrams

Stock control can be aided by using a **stock-control diagram** to measure the level of stock over time.

> **Stock-control diagram** Measures the level of stock over time.

An example stock-control diagram is shown in Figure 9 and is interpreted as follows:

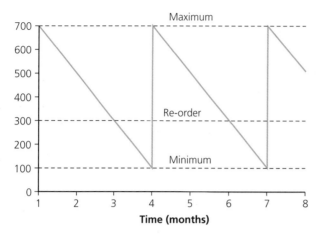

Figure 9 Example of a stock-control diagram

- **Stock level** is the solid line showing different levels of stock held at any one time. As stock is used, the level falls from left to right, for example when products are purchased. When more deliveries of stock are made, the line rises.
- **Maximum stock level** represents the maximum amount of stock that the firm wants to hold at any one time.
- **Reorder level** is the trigger to the stock-control system. Once stocks reach this level then an automatic re-supply order is generated and communicated to suppliers. This is because the supplier will need some **lead time** to process and make the delivery.
- **Buffer stock** or **minimum stock level** is the reserve level of stock, which is held just in case there is a problem. Holding buffer stock will help the business avoid running out of stock if the supplier takes longer than the normal lead time to resupply. However, holding buffer stock requires extra factory or shop space as well as the cost of holding the stock.
- In Figure 9 the buffer stock is set at 100 and the reorder level is 300. The first reorder was made in month 3 and took 1 month to arrive, at which time the 100 buffer stock point was reached. The reorder amount was the maximum stock (700) minus the buffer stock (100) which means 600 units were delivered by the supplier in month 4.
- In reality stock-control diagrams will have many more fluctuations than the perfect lines shown in Figure 9. Different markets will require different levels of buffer stocks and suppliers have to be significantly more reliable and sensitive to reorder requests or the business will not meet its reorder requirements quickly enough and there will be no stock left for customers to purchase.

The impact of too much or too little stock on the business

Poor stock control can result in too much or too little stock. **Stock out** means the business has no stock. This means a loss of production and the potential loss of sales and reputation for the business.

Lead time The total time it takes to manufacture and/or deliver a product.

Exam tip

You will not have to draw a stock-control diagram but be prepared to comment on what the diagram is saying about a business's stock management.

Knowledge check 29

Why might a business selling fresh food want a very small amount of buffer stock?

Exam tip

Always consider the type of product and how it is purchased when evaluating stock levels in a question.

Overstocking means the business has too much buffer stock or has overestimated the level of demand so is holding too much stock. The implications include increased warehouse/shop space needed to store the stock, possible damage of stored stock, and money spent on security and insuring the stock against loss.

Research and development (R&D)

Innovation within a business will not happen only through the entrepreneur but also through employees and other people linked to the business.

Research and development (R&D) is defined as the investigation, invention and development of products including their testing, feedback and launch.

Product design

Good product design adds value and builds brand image and loyalty. As discussed earlier, three elements work together to create the design mix, as follows:

- **function:** how effectively the product works
- **aesthetics:** how it appeals to customers in terms of how it looks, feels or smells
- **costs of creating the product:** the costs involved in its manufacture and production

Focusing on R&D may help a business achieve the following:

- improved products that have higher added value
- a competitive advantage through novel designs and product features
- premium pricing, to operate increasing profit margins

The drawbacks of focusing on R&D include:

- the upfront costs are high before any return has been realised
- products may be developed that customers do not want or are out of date due to changes in customer preferences

Economies of scale

Economies of scale are the savings in costs a business can make by expanding its level of production, thus reducing average costs.

Internal economies of scale are a function of the growing size of an individual business and include:

- **Technical economies of scale**, where the larger the business, the more it can afford to invest in specialist machinery and automation.
- **Specialisation**, where the larger the workforce, the more production can be split into different activities in order to raise productivity.
- **Purchasing economies of scale**, where the larger the business, the more power it has to bulk-order materials and products at discounted prices.
- **Managerial economies of scale**, where specialists are employed by large manufacturers to supervise production, marketing and human resources.

External economies of scale are a result of a whole industry growing in size and thus being able to reduce costs. For example, as the number of smartphones sold globally increased from 10 million to 100 million, suppliers of key components were able to reduce their unit costs.

Innovation The process of translating an idea or invention into a good or service that creates value for which customers will pay.

Research and development (R&D) The investigation, invention and development of products including their testing, feedback and launch.

Economies of scale Savings a business can make by increasing its level of production, which can reduce its average costs.

Internal economies of scale Relate to the growth of an individual business.

External economies of scale A result of a whole industry growing in size.

External economies of scale include:

- **Research and development**, where facilities in universities can help businesses innovate in the creation and development of their products.
- **Relocation of suppliers of parts** closer to manufacturers to produce cost savings. For example, Formula 1 parts suppliers are mainly located in the Midlands, where the manufacturers of F1 cars such as McLaren are located.
- **Investment in industry-related infrastructure**, such as high-speed data networks for the Silicon Valley software industry.

Diseconomies of scale

Diseconomies of scale occur when managerial inefficiencies put upwards pressure on costs per unit. This can occur due to:

- **Poor internal communication** between different departments and along the chain of command, resulting in less clear instructions, mistakes and therefore lower productivity.
- **Poor employee motivation**, which might be the result of workers feeling isolated and/or less appreciated, in which case their loyalty and productivity may decline.
- **Overtrading**, which is where a business suffers financial difficulties from growing too quickly. This particularly relates to cash flow—if a business expands too quickly, it might not have enough money to purchase raw materials to meet the demands of higher sales.

The survival of small firms

Instead of pursuing growth and economies of scale, businesses may decide that their objectives are best met by remaining comparatively small, like Bristol Cars, the manufacturer of hand-built sports cars. Some benefits of staying small include:

- **Product differentiation and unique selling points**, which can be the key to the success of some small businesses. For example, a business might be known for exceptional personal service and this might be lost if the business moves towards the mass market.
- **Flexibility in responding to customer needs**. Responding rapidly to changing customer needs is normally achieved by having a flat management structure as can be seen in Figure 10.
- **Providing excellent customer service**, which may be easier to achieve in a small business in which staff can more easily see the positive contribution they are making to the business.
- **E-commerce**, which can create successful small businesses that would find it difficult to succeed otherwise.

> **Exam tip**
>
> Businesses do not always have a choice as to which approach they use for growth. This can come down to factors outside their control, such as the speed at which opportunities arise in the market. Every business faces different circumstances.

> **Knowledge check 30**
>
> How does a business such as a Premier League football club achieve increased economies of scale? Give an example of how this could benefit them financially.

> **Exam tip**
>
> It is a trap in business to think that growth is always good. In reality businesses often succeed initially due to their unique product or service and small size but many lose these strengths when they grow. You could conclude that growth risks being self-destructive if not managed very carefully.

Figure 10 Small firms have fewer management layers between the top and bottom of the structure

The impact of economies and diseconomies of scale on a business and its stakeholders

Positive impacts:

- The larger the business becomes, the more it will benefit from economies of scale, reducing average unit costs.
- The lower the unit costs, the greater the potential profit margin, or the business can undercut its competitors to gain market share.
- Shareholders benefit from greater profitability, a higher share price related to the growth of the business and an increase in dividend payments.

Negative impacts:

- The larger the business, the higher the risk of suffering from diseconomies of scale. For example, becoming so big they lose their ability to respond rapidly to market changes which ultimately can lead to losses in market share and profit.
- Large businesses can dominate a market so much that they adopt monopolistic tendencies and come under scrutiny from competition authorities. In 2017 Google received a $2.7 billion fine from the European Union for favouring its own shopping services in search results, due to their market dominance.
- Business can often lose sight of the customer and their wants and needs, resulting in dissatisfaction, loss of sales and lower profits.

Content Guidance

Summary

After studying this topic, you should be able to:

- explain, calculate and evaluate added value
- explain and evaluate different methods of production
- explain, calculate and evaluate labour productivity and capacity utilisation
- explain and evaluate new technology in production and lean production
- explain and evaluate different methods of manging quality and methods of stock control
- explain, interpret and evaluate a stock control diagram
- explain and evaluate research and development, economies and diseconomies of scale and why firms may decide to remain small

Questions & Answers

The questions and answers in this section of the book follow a similar structure to your exams. There are extracts from business situations, data and a selection of all the different types of question you will be asked to answer either in the WJEC or WJEC Eduqas AS exam or WJEC Eduqas A-level exam.

Immediately below each question there are some examiner tips on how best to approach it (indicated by the icon ⓔ).

For each question there is both a lower-grade answer (Student A) and an upper-grade answer (Student B). The commentary that follows each answer (indicated by the icon ⓔ) points out the answer's strengths and weaknesses, and how it could be improved.

Exam structure

The **WJEC AS** qualification consists of two papers which are worth a total of 140 marks. This guide focuses on Paper 2 which lasts 2 hours and is worth 80 marks. The paper consists of data-response questions. Questions are worth 2, 4, 6, 8, or 12 marks. Students must answer all the questions.

The **WJEC Eduqas AS** qualification consists of two papers which are worth a total of 130 marks. This guide focuses on Component 2 which lasts 2 hours and is worth 80 marks. Section A is worth 55 marks and Section B is worth 25 marks. The paper has structured questions which are worth 2, 3, 4, 6, 8, 10 or 15 marks, and an essay-style question from a choice of three.

The **WJEC Eduqas A-level** qualification has three papers which are worth a total of 240 marks. This guide focuses on part of Component 1 which lasts 2 hours 15 minutes and is worth 80 marks. The paper consists of compulsory short-answer question in section A and compulsory data-response questions in section B. The paper has structured questions which are worth 2, 3, 4, 6, 8 or 12 marks. Students must answer all the questions.

This guide will only cover questions related to Business Functions. For questions on Business Opportunities please refer to *WJEC/Eduqas AS/A-level Year 1 Business Student Guide 1: Business opportunities*, also in this series.

Exam skills

For the 2-mark and 3-mark questions knowledge of business terms is required. These questions may also ask you to calculate answers using formulae you have learned and data in the extract material.

Questions worth 4 or 6 marks require knowledge of business terms, specific application of the business term from the extract material and an advantage and/or disadvantage of the business term related to the extract material. These questions may also ask you to calculate answers using formulae you have learned and data in the extract material. The examiner will mark this type of question 'from the bottom up'. This means that each mark is earned individually, so you will get marks for an advantage, for example, even if you have not provided any context from the extract material. Context is anything unique you discuss from the extract in your answer. It must relate back to question.

Questions worth 8, 10, 12 or 15 marks require evaluation of the business term using specific evidence from the extract. The safest way to do this is to produce a strong, two-sided argument. You should also aim to make judgements about the business and the key terms discussed, together with proposing solutions to business problems based on the stimulus material and your business knowledge. The examiner will mark these types of question from a 'best fit' point of view. This means that examiners will give you marks for the highest level of response you show in your answer. For the 8-mark question, to obtain full marks two reasons/factors need to be discussed with a two-sided argument, though the level of detail expected will be less than for the 10, 12 or 15-mark questions. It is worth emphasising the statement at the top level (AO4) of WJEC Eduqas mark schemes:

> Evaluate quantitative and qualitative information to make informed judgements and propose evidence-based solutions to business issues.

Technique when evaluating 12- or 15-mark questions

As these are the most challenging answers to write on the paper the examiner is looking for some detailed evaluation. To help you gain the highest AO4 marks it may help to consider one of the following issues in your evaluation, known as MOPS, which stands for:

- **Market.** What are the characteristics of the market in which the business operates? How do these influence your conclusion? For example, Apple is in the smartphone market which is dynamic and fast changing and therefore requires a lot money to be spent on research and development to ensure it keeps its competitive advantage.
- **Objectives.** What are the objectives of the business? How do the business's objectives align to the situation in which it finds itself? How does this influence your conclusion? For example, Apple's objective might be market share, so being the most novel product regardless of cost may be of the greatest importance.
- **Product.** What products or services does the business sell? How might this influence your thinking? For example, Apple may bring out a cheaper iPhone in garish colours to capture more market share.
- **Situation.** What is the current situation the business finds itself in? Does this affect your conclusion? For example, with sales of smartphones peaking Apple needs to find an extension strategy, such as selling to other global markets (e.g. India) to maintain/improve market share, hence the need for a cheaper phone.

You need to read the extract and the question, and use the most appropriate element(s) of MOPS in this context to help look at the wider issues affecting the business that will influence the key issues in the question.

1 WJEC AS

HMV, the records to multimedia high-street chain, is staging a dramatic fightback less than 4 years after it was saved from collapse by the venture capitalist firm Hilco. From £170 million of debt in 2013, the business has been restructured, reducing its shops from 223 to 140 outlets.

Accounts for January to December 2013 show the chain made £16 million of operating profit on £311.2 million of sales. The performance points to an impressive turnaround in the face of competition from the tech giants Amazon and Apple and the supermarkets. HMV now has a 16.6% share of the multimedia market in the UK, second only to Amazon on 23.1%.

According to Hilco, all the stores are now profitable thanks to a large-scale restructuring programme and the introduction of financial and non-financial incentives for employees. Debts and central costs have been cut dramatically. For example, HMV has centralised its stock ordering in London to reduce the amount of faulty items being sent to stores, and store rents and supplier terms have been renegotiated. It has also changed its store layouts to make it easier to accommodate customer experiences such as band visits and signing days. The online shop has been redesigned so that orders can be delivered within a day, with its cross-platform app, with prices matching or undercutting competitors, thereby boosting sales. The renaissance of vinyl has also had a positive effect on HMV, increasing the number of customers visiting stores. A unique streaming app for both music and video is in development.

Operating profit

Define what is meant by operating profit. (2 marks)

ⓔ The 'define' command word means you need to give a definition of the business term in the question and this needs to be clear.

AO1: for understanding what the business term used means. This is worth up to 2 marks and can include an enhanced definition or a basic definition. Accurate definitions are critical to gain marks.

Student A

Operating profits at HMV are £16 million. ⓐ

ⓔ **0/2 marks awarded.** ⓐ The student has attempted to relate a relevant part of the extract to the business term, but has not related this to the definition and has not even been specific as to where in the extract this figure is taken from, so gains no marks.

Student B

Operating profit is how much profit has been made in total from the trading activities of the business before any account is taken of how the business is financed. ⓐ Operating profit = gross profit − other operating expenses. ⓑ

ⓔ **2/2 marks awarded.** ⓐ The student has given a precise definition of operating profit for 1 AO1 mark. ⓑ The student has then given the formula to calculate operating profit which also gains 1 AO1 mark.

For Student A to score 0 marks (U grade) shows a lack of preparation and understanding of the skills needed to answer the question. Student B shows an excellent knowledge of both the definition and formula of operating profit to achieve full marks.

Financial and non-financial methods of motivation

To what extent do you agree with the view that financial and non-financial methods of motivating employees had the greatest impact on HMV's success? (8 marks)

ⓔ The 'to what extent' and 'do you agree' command phrases mean you need to provide a thorough assessment of the evidence on both sides of the argument, i.e. advantages and disadvantages with evaluation. You should create an extract-based answer discussing the advantages and disadvantages of the business concept. You also need to give a conclusion and make a judgement about the business term in the context of the stimulus material and include other relevant business theories. The extract can be used to provide application.

AO2: for applying methods of financial and non-financial motivation in the context of HMV. You should use application from the context correctly. This is worth up to 2 marks.

AO3: for giving a good analysis of the different financial and non-financial methods of motivating HMV employees, which should be balanced, detailed, well reasoned and developed. This is worth up to 2 marks.

AO4: for giving an excellent and balanced evaluation of how great an impact financial and non-financial methods of motivating staff has had on HMV's success. The advantages and disadvantages should be balanced and focused on the key issue. Judgements should be made with supporting comments and weight attached to the value of the points made. This is worth up to 4 marks.

> ### Student A
>
> Financial incentives are methods of paying employees in order to motivate them to achieve the objectives of the business. ⓐ One method of financially motivating staff at HMV could have been a bonus, an extra payment made to recognise the contribution made to a business for achieving a target. ⓑ This could be giving employees a target of how many sales they should achieve in a week or month and if they achieve this they will receive an extra payment above their usual wage. ⓒ HMV is said to have become profitable by using financial incentives with employees so clearly this means it must have had a positive impact on the success of HMV. ⓓ However, the text also says non-financial incentives were part of the HMV's success ⓔ. Non-financial methods include teamworking and empowerment, where official authority is given to employees to make decisions and control their own activities. ⓕ An advantage of empowerment and teamworking is there is less financial cost to the business as they usually

motivate staff who want greater decision-making in the workplace. g Therefore non-financial incentives are much cheaper for a business to use to improve employee performance and will have played as big a role in helping HMV become successful. h In conclusion, it is likely that both financial and non-financial motivation contributed equally to HMV's success. i

🄴 **4/8 marks awarded.** a b The student has recalled the definitions of financial incentives and bonus but as there are no marks awarded for knowledge this gains no marks. c d The student has given a limited contextual example of how a bonus may work with staff at HMV for 1 AO2 mark. A limited benefit of the use of a bonus is related to HMV's success for 1 AO3 mark. e f The student uses the context to state that non-financial rewards may also have contributed to HMV's success and defines two types. However, as the context used is weak and there are no marks for knowledge this gain no marks. g h The student gives a benefit of using non-financial methods of motivating staff and gives limited evaluation of non-financial compared to financial methods for 1 AO3 and 1 AO4 mark. i The student attempts to make a conclusion but as it is very generic and makes assumptions it gain no further marks.

Student B

Financial incentives such as commission may have had the greatest impact on HMV's success as this would encourage staff in the 140 stores to promote CDs to customers. a This is because for every extra CD they sell they would receive a percentage of the sale in commission, thus acting as a motivator to employees to increase revenue across the chain and is possibly one of the reasons HMV is not only profitable but also has a large market share of 16.6%. b However, HMV seemed to be struggling when they were taken over so Hilco may not have had the funds available to offer commission to staff—after all, out of 223 stores there are now only 140 left. c It may be more likely that HMV's success was down to non-financial motivators, playing to Herzberg's theory of motivation that suggests job enrichment and empowerment will produce the best performance in employees. d As it appears that the structure of the business has had to be altered dramatically it is likely that with a flatter organisation non-financial methods of motivation will have been used to improve the performance of staff and stores e. Empowerment of managers may have allowed them to react to local situations with little consultation with HMV headquarters, such as changing a store layout to suit an area where vinyl is more popular than CDs. f As staff in HMV stores tend to be passionate about music and multimedia they may have reacted more positively to issues that encouraged self-actualisation rather than simply wanting a carrot-and-stick approach, such as commission. g This may have led to staff feeling more valued, as they were able to take part in the local decision-making process leading to increased motivation, improved productivity, better customer care and increased sales revenues. h However, it may have been a combination of factors such as better branding, more market orientation such as increased vinyl sales and significant cost cutting that may have had the greatest impact on HMV's success, though it must be remembered that underpinning all such changes is a necessity to have motivated and innovative staff. i

🅔 **8/8 marks awarded.** 🅐 and 🅑 The student used good context to analyse why financial motivators may have had the greatest impact on HMV's success for 1 AO2 and 1 AO3 mark. 🅒–🅔 The student gives a detailed evaluation of why non-financial motivators may have had the greatest impact on HMV's success with good use of context for 1 AO4 and 1 AO2 mark. 🅕–🅗 The student uses the context to state in detail how non-financial rewards may be more likely to have had the greatest impact on HMV's success with excellent analysis for 1 AO3 mark and 1 AO4 mark. 🅘 The student then evaluates financial and non-financial motivators in the context of the wider business with clear understanding of a number of other factors that may have led to HMV's success, while making a set of judgements including the importance of staff for 2 AO4 marks.

Student A's answer shows a lack of understanding of the question, though there is basic understanding and analysis of issues for a D grade. Student B gives a well-balanced and methodical evaluation of not only financial and non-financial motivators in the context of the business, but also links this to relevant motivational theories and the wider business situation, providing insightful judgements, well worth an A*.

Distribution channels

To what extent do you agree with the view that offering varied methods of distribution to its customers will guarantee the long-term success for HMV? (12 marks)

🅔 The 'to what extent' and 'do you agree' command phrases mean you need to provide a thorough assessment of the evidence on both sides of an argument, i.e. advantages and disadvantages with evaluation. You should create an extract-based answer discussing the advantages and disadvantages of the business concept. You also need to give a conclusion and make a judgement about the business term in the context of the stimulus material and include other relevant business theories. The extract can be used to provide application.

AO1: for knowledge and understanding of the business term in the question, such as a definition for distribution in detail. This is worth up to 2 marks.

AO2: for good application of examples of distribution methods used in the context of HMV. You should use application from the context correctly. This is worth up to 2 marks.

AO3: for giving a good analysis of the varied distribution channels used by HMV. The analysis should be balanced, detailed, well reasoned and developed. This is worth up to 2 marks.

AO4: for giving an excellent evaluation of the likely impacts of varied distribution channels on HMV. The advantages and disadvantages should be balanced and focused on the key issue. Judgements should be made with supporting comments and weight attached to the value of the points made. This is worth up to 6 marks.

Student A

Place is known as distribution, and is about how a business gets its products to the customers. a This can be done through distribution channels such as retailer to customer, with HMV being the retailer in this scenario. b One advantage of HMV having different methods of distribution is that customers can buy their products where it is convenient for them. c For example, customers can buy a record from an HMV store or order it on their mobile to be delivered to their home address. d By having a number of distribution channels to customers HMV can satisfy a wider audience's needs and make more sales. e This will result in an increase in sales and an increase in profit from their 2013 operating profit of £311.2 million. f However, having a large number of distribution channels will mean HMV having large costs which could mean lower profits overall. g

e **6/12 marks awarded.** a and b The student has recalled a definition of distribution and has developed this for 2 AO1 marks. The student has also gained 1 AO2 mark for correctly relating the context of HMV to distribution. c The student has given a basic advantage to HMV of having more than one distribution channel for 1 AO3 mark. d The advantage is correctly developed to gain a further analysis mark of 1 AO3 mark. e and f The student develops the advantage further with good use of context to gain 1 AO2 mark. As analysis marks have reached their maximum, no further credit can be given for this analysis. g The student attempts to give a disadvantage of having a larger number of distribution channels but this is superficial and shows no evaluation so gains no further mark or level.

Student B

One advantage of HMV offering a number of methods of distribution to customers is that it is likely to satisfy the wants and needs of a wider audience, for example those who wish to visit shops for the experience of a band signing and those that just want to order music on their mobile phone and receive it at home. a As a consequence of this wider audience HMV are able to differentiate themselves from Amazon and Apple, who offer no physical music stores and this has clearly been a positive factor in the 'turnaround' of HMV by Hilco, to its current market share of 16.6%. b HMV is also looking at expanding its distribution channels to include a music and video app, which may further strengthen its market share so that it continues to innovate based on the preferences of customers for novel methods of product delivery. c As a result, operating profits are likely to continue improving from their 2013 figure of £311.2 million. d

However, continually expanding distribution channels will cost HMV in both the research and development and the staff needed to continually update IT systems. e Offering a 1-day delivery service, for example, is likely to be very expensive compared to normal postal deliveries, meaning running costs may start to reduce HMV's profit margins on sales of items such as CDs and LPs. f As a consequence overall profits may suffer in the longer term and if HMV does not keep a close eye on costs it runs the risk of amassing losses and if this persists, closures, such as happened in January 2013. g HMV also needs to be wary of issues such as price, as Amazon and Apple may be able to make more money from selling electronic downloads than physical sales. h The key to continued success for HMV is to continue to innovate and offer unique experiences for customers, such as band signings in stores, while remaining price and cost competitive across all distribution methods. i The streaming app, for example, must offer some innovations to customers such as exclusive band music and pre-released films in order to gain a competitive advantage and ensure profit margins and market share continue to grow successfully. j This way HMV can guarantee its long term success through not only varied distribution channels but its overall marketing mix offering. k

e 12/12 marks awarded. a The student has given an advantage of HMV having numerous distribution methods with good contextual examples for 2 AO1 marks and 2 AO2 marks. b The benefit is explained in detail using evidence from the context for 1 AO3 mark. c and d The student further develops the impact of different distribution channels for 1 AO3 mark. e – g The student evaluates the effect of expanding distribution channels on HMV with a good use of contextual evidence and development for 2 AO4 marks. h and i The student then evaluates the importance of distribution in the context of the marketing mix with a good use of evidence for 2 AO4 marks. j The student also evaluates and suggests a solution for HMV to innovate its products and distribution channels with context for 1 AO4 mark. k A conclusion is reached referring to the importance of distribution channels in the context of the marketing mix for 1 AO4 mark.

Student A manages to gain half marks (a D grade) by making reasonable use of evidence combined with their knowledge of distribution channels, with some benefits. However, the answer fails to make any attempt at an evaluation or judgement. Student B uses the stimulus material well to give a benefit and a risk in context and develops their points well. The answer shows a wide understanding of distribution channels and evaluates them against the marketing mix for HMV, giving a reasoned judgement and conclusion for full marks and an A grade.

2 WJEC Eduqas AS

Extract

J D Wetherspoon started life in 1979 and become a plc in 1992. It now has 750 pubs which also serve food, and is the second largest pub chain in the UK. One of its reasons for success is that the pubs combine cheap food and drinks with opening hours that run from late breakfast to midnight. The business has aggressive growth targets in terms of opening new venues and product sales.

Profits reported to 24 January 2016 before tax were £36 million, down 3.8% compared to 12 months before. However, revenues for the same period increased to £790.3 million. This was partly down to diseconomies of scale, higher staff costs such as rises in the minimum wage and also because pubs tend to pay more tax on alcohol than that bought from competitors such as supermarkets.

Wetherspoon has 35,000 employees, with most of them working in its pubs. The company tries to ensure some of its staff are recruited from the long-term unemployed, ex-armed forces and those with disabilities. Sixty-two per cent of staff are under 25. A lot of them have not been in employment before. Managers of pubs are employed by Wetherspoon for an average of 10.5 years. Around 18% of employees, known as 'associates', stay with the business for 3 years or more. Employee turnover is at its lowest since the business started. Associates are on zero hours contracts with no guaranteed work each week, but they are able to work for other employers and to refuse any hours offered. Only managers have minimum working hours each week, although associates can apply for this under certain circumstances.

Diseconomies of scale

With reference to the 'diseconomies of scale' propose three possible solutions to solve these problems faced by J D Wetherspoon. (3 marks)

(e) The 'propose' command word means you need to recommend a solution that is based on a supported reason. You should provide a course of action for the business with brief evidence.

AO4: for giving a recommendation to address the diseconomies of scale issues affecting J D Wetherspoon. Proposals should be made with supporting comments and brief evidence. This is worth up to 3 marks.

Student A

Diseconomies of scale occur when managerial inefficiencies put upwards pressure on costs per unit. a

(e) **0/2 marks awarded.** a The student has given an accurate definition of diseconomies of scale, but as this does not answer the question the student gains no marks.

Student B

One problem J D Wetherspoon may be facing is overtrading, due to the fact the business has aggressive growth targets. a A solution might be to reduce the number of new pubs Wetherspoon is opening so that it can ensure cash flow is able to keep up with the purchasing of raw materials such as beer and wine, allowing pubs to supply the demand for drink, increasing cash and ultimately profits. b

Another problem may be that poor employee motivation is affecting productivity, as the extract states most staff are on contracts with no guaranteed hours. c A solution may be that staff are offered guaranteed hours, giving them more job security, greater motivation enhancing productivity at the 750 venues. d

A final problem may be poor internal communication as there are 750 different pubs spread across the whole of the UK. e If each manager has to order stock from a central office it may be that the orders are not communicated either clearly or quickly enough to arrange for delivery in time. f A solution may be to have a computerised stock control system that automatically registers each sale and orders products when a buffer stock is reached. g

ⓔ **3/3 marks awarded.** a and b The student identifies a problem using evidence and then proposes a clearly explained solution for 1 AO4 mark. c and d The student identifies another problem and gives another clearly explained solution for 1 AO4 mark. e–g A final problem and a detailed solution are proposed and explained for 1 AO4 mark.

For Student A to score 0 marks (U grade) shows a lack of preparation and understanding of the skills needed to answer the question. Student B shows an excellent understanding of diseconomies of scale in the context of the business, giving clear proposals for improvement, gaining an A grade.

Management by objectives

Explain two benefits to a business such as Wetherspoon of adopting a management by objectives approach to its business.   (6 marks)

ⓔ The 'explain' command word means you need to provide details and reasons as to how and why something is the way it is. Your answer should show the meaning of what you are being asked to explain, and it should explain the impact, positive or negative, of the business term on the business.

AO1: for naming two benefits of management by objectives. This is worth a maximum of 2 marks.

AO2: for applying each benefit to a business such as Wetherspoon. You should use application correctly and provide appropriate evidence from the context. This is worth up to 2 marks.

AO3: for a full analysis of the benefits of management by objectives in the context of a business such as Wetherspoon.

To gain good marks two different benefits need to be identified and related to the context of the business.

Student A

Management by objectives (MBO) means improving the business performance through clearly defined objectives for managers and employees. **a** A benefit of MBO is that clear objectives allow for the measurement of performance and improvement at all levels of the organisation. **b** Wetherspoon could use MBO to set targets for how quickly staff serve customers a drink at the bar and then discuss with staff how to improve this target. **c** A drawback is that the objectives set may not be SMART: specific, measurable, achievable, relevant and timely. **d** For example, if McDonald's set a very quick target for staff to take orders for food such as within 15 seconds of a customer entering the restaurant, then in busy times this would be unachievable. **e** This means the objective is impossible to meet, possibly causing staff to feel demotivated and therefore affecting productivity. **f**

---

e **2/6 marks awarded.** **a** The student gives a definition of management by objectives (MBO) but as the question asks for benefits, this gains no credit. **b** The student gives a benefit of MBO for 1 AO1 mark. **c** They then give a contextual benefit of adopting MBO for 1 AO2 mark. **d** The student fails to answer the question by giving a drawback rather than a benefit, gaining no marks. **e** and **f** The student gives a good contextual analysis of the drawback in the context of McDonald's but again gains no credit as it fails to answer the question regarding the impact on Wetherspoon.

Student B

Management by objectives (MBO) means improving the business performance through clearly defined objectives for managers and employees. A benefit of MBO is that clear objectives allow for the measurement of performance and improvement at all levels of the organisation. **a** Wetherspoon could use MBO to set targets for how quickly staff serve customers and then discuss with staff how to improve this target, in order to further increase turnover from £790.3 million in 2016. **b** With staff targets set at a challenging but achievable level for taking orders, customer service would improve and may help Wetherspoon to improve customer satisfaction and gain repeat purchases. **c**

Another benefit of MBO is that if managers encourage staff to participate in the setting of their objectives this may empower them, creating a more motivated set of workers and higher levels of achievement across Wetherspoon pubs. **d** As many staff at Wetherspoon are on zero hours contracts, encouraging staff to be involved in setting their own objectives will encourage greater teamwork, higher levels of motivation and potentially higher productivity as a result. **e** This would help make the aggressive growth targets for sales and opening new venues more likely to be achieved while maintaining high levels of customer service, resulting in improved levels of revenue and profit. **f**

ⓔ 6/6 marks awarded. **ⓐ** The student gives a benefit of MBO gaining 1 AO1 mark. **ⓑ** and **ⓒ** The student develops in detail the benefit with excellent use of context regarding the positive effects this may have on Wetherspoon's business for 1 AO2 mark and 1 AO3 mark. **ⓓ** The student then gives a further benefit of MBO for 1 AO1 mark **ⓔ** and **ⓕ** The student develops the benefit in detail with excellent use of the context of Wetherspoon for 1 AO2 mark and 1 AO3 mark.

Student A makes a number of errors typical of students who fail to read the question carefully. There is significant wasted effort on a definition and what is good analysis that fails to answer the question. This student clearly has a good understanding of MBO but is let down by their exam technique (E grade). Student B displays excellent skills in applying detailed analysis of MBO to the context of Wetherspoon, with excellent use of appropriate context (an A* grade).

Labour turnover

Evaluate the importance of minimising labour turnover for a business such as Wetherspoon. (10 marks)

ⓔ The 'evaluate' command word means you need to write an extract-based answer discussing the advantages and disadvantages of the business concept. You also need to make a judgement about the business term in the context of the extract and include other relevant business theories.

AO1: for good understanding of why minimising labour turnover is important to Wetherspoon or a definition of labour turnover. This is worth a maximum of 2 marks.

AO2: for good application of why minimising labour turnover is important to Wetherspoon. You should make clear reference to the extract to support your argument. This is worth up to 2 marks.

AO3: for good, clear analysis of how the identified issues are important for the success of Wetherspoon. This is worth up to 2 marks.

AO4: for a detailed and well-balanced evaluation of the key factors affecting labour turnover in the context of Wetherspoon. A supported judgement should be made about the business term in the context of the question, possibly with a recommendation about the best strategy. This is worth up to 4 marks.

Student A

Labour turnover is defined as the ability of a firm to convince its employees to remain with the business. **a** A benefit of low labour turnover is that the business will have lower selection and training costs than competitors as it will not need to advertise for new staff as much. **b** This means that Wetherspoon will make a greater profit margin from each drink it sells. **c** The extract states that labour turnover is at its lowest so this means the costs of labour turnover have improved from previous years. **d**

However, if labour turnover is too low the business could miss out on the benefits of new staff coming to the business. **e** These include bringing new ideas to the business and new staff being able to challenge current methods of working. **f** For example, a new member of staff could have worked at a competitor's which had a more efficient method of serving drinks. **g**

Labour turnover needs to be low so costs are reduced as much as possible in the business. **h**

e **6/12 marks awarded.** **a** The student gives a definition of labour turnover for 1 AO1 mark. **b** The student gives a benefit of low labour turnover which is developed but is not related to a business so only gains 1 AO3 mark. **c** and **d** The student then gives a benefit of low labour turnover to Wetherspoon, showing an understanding of how this may have contributed to Wetherspoon's success, with relevant context, for 1 AO2 mark and 1 AO3 mark. **e–g** The student presents a problem of minimising labour turnover and gives an example relevant to Wetherspoon for 1 AO1 mark and 1 AO2 mark. As the analysis is not well developed there would be no credit for this, although this student has already gained the maximum AO3 marks. **h** The student attempts to make a recommendation but as it lacks any development it gains no further marks.

Student B

One important reason for Wetherspoon to minimise labour turnover is that profits for 2016 are down 3.8% . **a** As labour costs are one of the biggest costs of a business, minimising labour turnover will mean Wetherspoon will keep more staff and so reduce costs such as that spent on selection and training. **b** Wetherspoon has managed to retain 18% of its staff for over 3 years and further methods that encourage increased labour retention can only help to reduce costs further. **c** Another reason to minimise labour turnover would be that the longer staff stay in their job, the more efficient they will become and the likely result is that customer service in the pubs will improve. **d** This will both enhance customers' experience of the pub and encourage customer loyalty and greater customer spending on visits. **e** This should lead to greater profit margins and reduce the impact on profits of the national minimum wage. **f**

However, minimising labour turnover will need to be considered in the context of the industry norms. [g] For example, if competitors keep 18% of their staff for over 5 years then clearly Wetherspoon has not put sufficient strategies in place to retain staff. [h] As a consequence costs of selection and training of new staff will be higher than competitors'. [i] Wetherspoon may also be missing out on the benefits of higher labour turnover such as new staff bringing new ideas which may increase productivity [j] For example, new staff would be able to pass on new ideas about unique beers that could be incorporated into Wetherspoon's offering to produce a USP that would more than cover the costs of the labour turnover and ultimately lead to further innovation and a competitive advantage. [k]

The key to minimising labour turnover for Wetherspoon is to ensure that it is significantly better than competitors, so as to reduce comparative costs. [l] According to the evidence pub managers stay for over 10 years so if Wetherspoon is serious about emulating this success then it needs to invest more money in giving staff guaranteed hours contracts, to those who want them. [m] This will create the best balance between allowing better retention and benefits such as better teamwork and customer service, and flexibility in the workforce which in the long term may become a clear competitive advantage to Wetherspoon and turn the current 3.8% reduction in profits to an increase. [n]

[e] 10/10 marks awarded. [a] The student gives a reason why labour turnover needs to be minimised, including evidence from the extract for 1 AO1 mark and 1 AO2 mark. [b] and [c] The student then gives an analysis with evidence of minimising labour turnover which has good development for 1 AO2 mark and 2 AO3 marks. [d]–[i] The student gives a further benefit of minimising labour turnover with evidence and analysis gaining 1 AO1 mark, all other marks for analysis and application having reached their maximum. [g]–[i] The student evaluates the minimisation of labour turnover from the perspective of competitor comparisons with good use of the extract, gaining 2 AO4 marks. [j] and [k] The student gives a further evaluative point with evidence for another AO4 mark. [l]–[n] A judgement and recommendation is then made on what Wetherspoon's approach should be to minimising labour turnover which gives the potential long-term benefits, gaining 1 AO4 mark.

Student A makes some use of the extract and gives analysis using evidence about the business concept but it is a little superficial in places and lacks depth. They fail to gain any marks for evaluation (D grade). Student B makes excellent use of a wide range of business concepts, including a detailed knowledge of the issues relating to labour turnover. They give a clear evaluation of the issues and a clear judgement related to MOPS, with some discussion as to how a strategy may work (A grade). However, this student could have achieved similar marks with a shorter answer, so remember to be careful not to run out of time towards the end of the paper.

3 WJEC Eduqas A-level

Extract 1

A new technology brand is attempting to convince London's super-rich to pay £10,000 or more for a smartphone with its first shop.

Sirin Labs, a start-up backed by $72 million (£50 million) of the chief executive Tal Cohen's own funding, investor loans and a large overdraft facility from Sirin's bank, is poised to launch the device into a crowded market in which Apple's iPhone dominates the high end.

Sirin will attempt to carve out a super-premium niche more than 10 times more expensive than an iPhone by using military-grade security features and premium materials, such as precious metals and diamonds. Yet the smartphone at its heart will be based on Google's Android operating system, which is available to mobile manufacturers free of charge. Sirin has managed to source parts for its smartphones for £50 per phone. The company hopes it can succeed in selling smartphones as status symbols in a specialised market where others have struggled, by making the phones to the customer's exact specifications. Cohen says the company is looking at a market size of 60 million, which includes 18 million millionaires. 'In every consumer market, about 2pc–10pc is high-end products. In mobiles, so far only 0.1pc–0.2pc of consumers have adopted high-end phones, so there should be at least another 1.8pc of this market attracted by a top-end product.'

Sirin Labs extract of assets for the month ending 30 June 2016

	£
Inventories (stocks)	50,000
Trade and other receivables	10,000
Cash at bank	500,000
Total current assets	560,000

Added value

Sirin has an order for a mobile phone of solid gold for which it is charging the customer £15,000. The cost of the precious metals used in the phone is £7,000 and other costs amount to £2,560.

Calculate the added value of the sale of the mobile phone to Sirin Labs. (3 marks)

e The 'calculate' command word means you must complete a calculation in stages using data from the extract. You should use the technique or formula that you have learned. It is important that you remember to include the appropriate unit(s) of measurement in your answers.

AO1: for knowledge and understanding of the business term in the question. This is worth 1 mark.

AO2: for good application, e.g. correctly applying the formula for calculating added value using the correct figures. This is worth up to 2 marks.

Student A

Added value means enhancing the gap between the production cost and the selling price. Customers can perceive the product as better than rivals' due to the brand image, enhancing brand loyalty. a Added value = selling price of product – cost of production b

e **1/3 marks awarded.** a The student gives an accurate definition of added value but as the question asks for a calculation this achieves no marks. b The student gives an accurate formula of added value for 1 AO1 mark.

Student B

Added value = selling price of product – cost of production. a

The cost of production = £7,000 + £2,560 = £9,560 b

Added value = £15,000 – £9,560 = £5,440 c

e **3/3 marks awarded.** a The student gives an accurate formula for added value for 1 AO1 mark. b The total costs of production are calculated for 1 AO2 mark. c The formula for added value is correctly used to calculate the answer for 1 AO2 mark.

Student A misunderstands the question and command word, gaining low marks (E grade). Student B gives a concise and well-presented answer with all three components for full marks (A* grade). You should easily achieve full marks for this style of question as long as you understand the command words and use the appropriate figures.

Stock control

Consider the view that poor stock control by a business such as Sirin Labs could lead to business failure.

(12 marks)

e The 'consider' command word means you need to review different information, opinions or perspectives in relation to the question. You should create an extract-based answer looking at the advantages and disadvantages of the business concept. You must also give a conclusion and make a judgement about the business term in the context of the stimulus material and include other relevant business theories. The extract can be used to provide application.

AO1: for knowledge and understanding of the business term in the question. This is worth up to 2 marks.

AO2: for good application showing examples of stock control used in the context of Sirin Labs. You should use application from the context correctly. This is worth up to 2 marks.

AO3: for giving an excellent analysis of poor stock control as a factor leading to the failure of the business. Your analysis should be balanced, detailed, well reasoned and developed. This is worth up to 4 marks.

AO4: for giving an excellent evaluation, which is well balanced, regarding the success or failure of the business in question due to poor stock control. The advantages and disadvantages should be balanced and focused on the key issues. Judgements should be made with supporting comments and weight attached to the value of the points made. This is worth up to 4 marks.

Student A

Stock control is the attempt by businesses to ensure that stock levels are managed efficiently. a The extract shows that Sirin Labs has £500 worth of stock. b Poor stock control will mean that the business has over-estimated how many mobile phones will be sold. c This means there will be an increase in costs for the business. d However Sirin Labs only has £500 worth of stock in June 2016 so this isn't a lot of stock and they will be able to sell it quickly in a busy place like London. e

---

e **3/10 marks awarded.** a The student gives an accurate definition of stock control to achieve 1 AO1 mark. b The student develops this point using relevant application but misinterprets the figures in the table so gains no marks. c The student gives a disadvantage of poor stock control with context gaining 1 AO3 mark and 1 AO2 mark. d The student develops their point to show an impact on the business but as it is generic and makes assumptions it gains no further marks. e The student then attempts to evaluate the stock situation for the business but as this is based on an incorrect interpretation of the data from the table it gains no marks.

Student B

Stock control is the attempt by the business to ensure that stock levels are managed efficiently; the stock level is simply the amount of stock held by a business. a The table of assets shows Sirin Labs is holding £50,000 of stock at the end of June 2016 and will have to pay out extra costs for the storage of this stock. b If Sirin's stock level is an example of overstocking, it means its forecasting of demand has been overestimated. c As a consequence it will have too much money tied up in stock and may not have enough working capital available to pay its current liabilities, for example the interest payable on the large overdraft facility Sirin's bank has allowed it in order to launch the business. d If this were to continue in the longer term, Sirin Labs would have cash flow problems and not be able to pay its debts, resulting in the business failing. e However, Sirin Labs is a new business which according to the case study has done research into the likely market for customers who will buy its £10,000 phones. f It has also raised a significant amount of funding (£50 million) so if poor stock control is simply down to a lack of historical data available about demand for phones then this is likely to improve as the business starts to sell in London. g As long as stock ordering becomes more realistic as the business gains sales, overstocking will become less of a problem as Sirin Labs can more accurately ensure it only has sufficient to meet demand. h As a consequence the £50,000 of stock held in June would reduce, lowering the extra costs of purchasing and holding such stock. i Therefore working capital would be available to pay for the mortgage and other costs. j In conclusion, Sirin Labs appears to have sufficient funds to cover any short-term problems with poor stock control. k

e 11/12 marks awarded. a The student gives an accurate definition of stock control, which is detailed enough for 2 AO1 marks. b The student then uses the data from the table to show a consequence of poor stock control for 1 AO3 mark and 1 AO2 mark. c and d The student gives a development of the consequence of these increased costs in context for 1 AO2 mark and 1 AO3 mark. e The consequence is developed further to show the impact of poor stock control on the business, gaining a further AO3 mark. f–h The student evaluates poor stock control using application in context, pointing out that Sirin Labs is a new business which has significant capital investment. The evaluation is developed to a logical conclusion, gaining 1 AO3 mark and 2 AO4 marks. i and j The student further develops the evaluation to reach a detailed conclusion for 1 AO4 mark. They go on to attempt a conclusion regarding poor stock control for Sirin Labs, but as it simply reiterates what has already been said and adds no judgement or recommendation, they gain no further marks.

Student A makes a common error and misinterprets the data in the table, missing out on marks that could easily have been gained with the correct interpretation (U grade). This limits the answer significantly even though there are higher level skills practised, such as using the extracts to answer the question. Student B makes excellent use of a wide range of business concepts, applying stock control and a wider knowledge of cash flow and working capital. There is excellent use of words like 'if' and 'could' to show they understand that outcomes can be unpredictable in the business environment, rather than using words like 'will' and 'would'.

The use of the data from the table and the business background from the case study are particularly well done, displaying a balanced and wide-ranging assessment of poor stock control. However, the conclusive point adds no further value to the answer. It would have been better if the student had suggested a method of reducing the possibility of poor stock control, such as using just-in time stock management or reducing buffer stocks. Still, an A* response.

Extract 2

Apple has posted its financial results for the second quarter of 2016. Revenue was down 12.8% ($50.6 billion). Compared with 2015, unit sales and revenues were down almost across the board. This appears to be down to low sales of iPhones with 51.2 million sold in 2016 compared with 61.2 million in 2015.

Analysts have blamed the downturn on a combination of factors including high market saturation, weak international currency, economic slowdown — particularly in China — and lacklustre sales of last September's iPhone 6s, which contained features analysts deemed too similar to the previous year's iPhone 6.

It is estimated that iPhone 6 costs roughly $230–$260 to manufacture, including accessories, shipping and packaging costs.

As a rule, consumers are upgrading their smartphones less frequently than in the past, leaving Apple in a tight spot should its annual release cycle fail to capture their attention.

Given the iPhone's status as Apple's most popular and lucrative product, the company will be pinning its hopes on the successful launch and reception of the iPhone 7.

Apple has been discussing its efforts to reduce waste by unveiling a robotic system it has developed called 'Liam', which can disassemble old iPhones and recover recyclable materials. Liam is capable of taking apart one iPhone every 11 seconds and will be installed in the US and Europe, eventually being able to deconstruct all iPhone models to recover resources. Up to 2015, the company had sold 700 million iPhones alone.

Apple is already recycling its own products and in 2015 was able to recover over 30 million kg of raw materials including 1,102 kg of gold.

Since 2007 manufacturers have had a legal obligation to ensure users can safely dispose of electrical products that are at the end of their useful life. If they do not meet this legal obligation they face unlimited fines. With this in mind, Apple operates Apple Renew, where customers can hand in their old iPhone and gain a credit towards their next phone.

Greenpeace welcomed Apple's initiative as a good example of the company's environmental commitments, but questioned how much impact the Liam robot would actually have on overall iPhone recycling volumes. The bulk of discarded iPhones go through independent e-waste recyclers, which will not have access to Liam.

Waste

Consider the view that minimising waste is important for the continued success of a business such as Apple.

(12 marks)

e The 'consider' command word means you need to review different information, opinions or perspectives in relation to the question. You should create an extract-based answer looking at the advantages and disadvantages of the business concept. You must also give a conclusion and make a judgement about the business term in the context of the stimulus material and include other relevant business theories. The extract can be used to provide application.

AO1: for knowledge and understanding of the business term in the question. This is worth up to 2 marks.

AO2: for good application showing examples of waste reduction in the context of Apple. You should use application from the context correctly. This is worth up to 2 marks.

AO3: for giving an excellent analysis of the importance of minimising waste as a factor in the continued success of the business. Your analysis should be balanced, detailed, well reasoned and developed. This is worth up to 4 marks.

AO4: for giving an excellent evaluation, which is well balanced, regarding the success or failure of the business in relation to waste minimisation. The advantages and disadvantages should be balanced and focused on the key issues. Judgements should be made with supporting comments and weight attached to the value of the points made. This is worth up to 4 marks.

Student A

Waste means anything that does not add value to the product. a A benefit of minimising waste is that it will reduce the costs of producing Apple's products. b This means that Apple will make a greater profit margin from each phone it sells. c Apple has taken the minimisation of waste to include recycling customers' old handsets by using its robot called Liam to take them apart. d This means that Apple can recycle these parts and turn them into new parts for new phones like the IPhone 7. e

However, Apple might be better off making phones that don't have any waste in the first place. f This could be done by using less raw materials in their construction which would mean there would be less cost to Apple, and Apple would still get the same benefit of being able to increase its profit margins. g

e **6/12 marks awarded.** a The student gives a definition of waste for 1 AO1 mark. b The student gives a benefit of reducing waste for 1 AO3 mark c The student attempts to give a consequence of minimising waste to Apple but as it is an assertion and generic it gains no further marks for AO3, but does gain 1 AO2 mark. d and e The student gives a contextual benefit of minimising waste and gives a basic benefit to Apple to gain 1 AO3 mark and 1 AO2 mark. f and g The student then attempts to evaluate the minimising of waste by suggesting a better and more cost-effective approach, but the points are generic and lack context so gain just 1 AO4 mark.

Student B

One important reason for Apple to minimise waste through recycling is because it has a legal obligation since 2007 to safely dispose of products customers no longer use. a With Apple producing 700 million iPhones this will mean it must find ways to safely dispose of all the phones that are out of date or broken and have created a robot to undertake this process. b By using Liam, Apple can not only meet its legal obligations, and avoid unlimited fines for not providing safe disposal of its phones for customers, but can also benefit from recovering a significant amount of valuable metals. c For example, Apple has already recovered 30 million kilograms of materials from old phones which can be sold or reused in new phones, reducing costs or creating another source of income. d

However, it would have been even more effective for Apple to minimise waste by using a more efficient method of production such as lean production which aims to minimise costs and enhance quality by using a range of waste-saving measures. ⓔ For example, Apple could use continuous improvement methods to try and minimise waste such as finding more eco-friendly materials to make its phones out of or just use less materials in the first place. ⓕ As a consequence waste would be minimised at the point of production rather than through recycling, meaning greater added value to the product and a reduction in the costs to make the phone, say from $230 down to $200. ⓖ This could mean higher profit margins as well as minimised waste for Apple. ⓗ

However, another important reason Apple may wish to reduce waste is to show its customers it takes its environmental responsibilities seriously. ⓘ By offering customers credit for their old iPhone and having the capability to recycle and reuse the old parts using the robot, customers may feel Apple's premium-priced products are good value due to their green credentials, encouraging customer loyalty, more sales and cheaper raw material costs for Apple due to the recycling program. ⓙ Apple should therefore continue with its recycling program to reuse waste and cut costs in the short term but should also consider more environmentally friendly methods of constructing handsets with the least waste in the longer term, to ensure customers continue to buy handsets. ⓚ

ⓔ **12/12 marks awarded.** ⓐ The student gives a reason Apple may wish to minimise waste with context for 1 AO1 mark and 1 AO2 mark. ⓑ–ⓓ The student then gives a consequence of minimising waste, which is in context and has good development, for 1 AO1 mark, 1 AO2 mark and 2 AO3 marks. ⓔ The student evaluates the minimisation of waste by suggesting it would be more efficient to do this through the production process for 2 AO3 marks. ⓕ–ⓗ The student develops this evaluation with good use of the extract to show a benefit of a different approach to minimising waste, gaining 2 AO4 marks. ⓘ ⓙ The student then offers a further evaluative point as to why recycling may be of benefit to Apple in terms of product sales and lower costs for 1 AO4 mark. ⓚ A judgement and a recommendation are made on how Apple may want to minimise waste in the short to long term, gaining 1 AO4 mark.

Student A makes some use of the extract and gives some analysis of the question but it is superficial and lacks depth, with some assertions, gaining only a D grade. Student B makes excellent use of a wide range of business concepts including a detailed knowledge of minimising waste in the broader context of production as well as recycling. The student also makes excellent use of the wider context of customer perceptions of recycling and the impact of these on sales, forming a reasoned recommendation and judgement. The answer takes a slightly different approach to evaluation in that it does not disagree with the question but takes the standpoint that waste minimisation can in fact be done even better than described in the extract, making for an insightful answer worth an A*.

Knowledge check answers

Knowledge check answers

1 Marks and Spencer's comprehensive database can only give details of historical buying habits rather than predicting what customers want in terms of future fashion. Without some method of predicting fashion trends and customer buying habits, the asset-led approach has limited benefits.

2 (a) Boeing: function and economic manufacture;
(b) Gucci: aesthetics and function;
(c) Barratt Homes: economic manufacture and function.

3 Apple has adopted an extension strategy for the iPhone 5s.

4 As the Boston matrix only works on market share and market growth, giving a snapshot of a product's performance at the time measured, it can only give an idea of whether it is performing well or not. It is the starting point for planning the next actions to be taken with a product. Further research and data will be needed to check whether the Boston matrix is a predictor of future market share and growth.

5 As Huawei is a new phone manufacturer it does not have the reputation and brand image to be able to sell its phones at the same price as Apple, due to the initial lack of customer demand. A lower price may tempt customers to try its new phone.

6 One that has a strong brand image.

7 Liverpool Football Club is sponsored by Subway.

8 Nike's brand is associated with the success of the famous footballer. Customers will associate his success with Nike's products and pay a premium to buy them.

9 As there is no business data for a new product, for example on sales, it will be almost impossible to create a budget based on past data.

10 When shareholders or investors want a dividend payment or the repayment of their investment.

11 New business start-ups which find it difficult to gain funding from other sources such as banks.

12 It has no historical data on which to base its predictions of sales and expenditure.

13 £500−(£150+£300) = £50

14 As the purchasers do not have to pay for the product straight away, they may actually delay payment longer than is allowed.

15 The gross profit margins are higher because the revenue from selling the food is much higher compared to the cost of raw materials than the revenue from just selling alcohol.

16 It is able to charge higher prices for its watches resulting in more profit.

17 Some businesses have to satisfy legal requirements in terms of staff skills. McDonald's will need to ensure all staff undertake some off-the-job training to gain basic qualifications in food safety and hygiene.

18 Because if there are more managers to supervise staff making food, the quality of the food should be better, meaning higher levels of customer satisfaction and ultimately more profit.

19 Employees will be encouraged to work as a team with managers listening to their ideas and opinions, thus encouraging creative ideas for new products.

20 If every worker benefited from any increased profits, it would be likely to motivate them to be more productive and give better customer service, leading to higher sales and profits.

21 Job rotation means employees from different roles taking on different jobs on the production line. Employees trying out a new task may spot working practices that could be improved using processes from other jobs they have carried out on the production line, thus improving quality overall.

22 Under laissez-faire leadership, employees are encouraged to make their own decisions within the boundaries set by the leader. Where leadership is autocratic, employees make no decisions, the leader has sole responsibility for making them.

23 Tesla is able to produce them at cost, rather than having to pay the added profit margin of another business. Tesla has predicted that costs per kWh of battery will be 30% to 40% less than if the batteries were bought from another manufacturer, which allows the company to keep the selling price at the current level while making more profit.

24 Because primark is a mass-market and low-cost clothes producer. Flow production allows for the most efficient and cheapest method of making such clothes.

25 In order to give more time to creating a higher quality product, for example tailor-made suits.

26 By improving its brand image or promoting products, for example by using special offers.

27 There may be new staff who need to be trained and who are not yet as efficient as more experienced staff.

28 By getting workers to look at their own roles and consider how they could do their work more quickly and efficiently, with less waste both of raw materials and time.

29 Any food not sold will be wasted and become an additional cost.

30 By increasing the size of its football ground to allow for a larger seating capacity. For example, Arsenal invested in the Emirates Stadium in 2006, which has a capacity of 60,432, allowing the club to sell seats in greater bulk and at much cheaper unit costs.

Note: **bold** page numbers indicate defined terms.

A

above-the-line promotion   **14**
absenteeism   **36**
accounting
   cash-flow forecasting   24–26
   income statement   26–28
   ratio analysis   29–30
added value   **7**
   calculation of   48–49
   questions and answers   75–76
   ways of increasing   49
advertising   14
Advisory, Conciliation and
   Arbitration Service
   (ACAS)   47
aesthetics of a product   8, 57
appraisal   **35**
apprenticeships   34
appropriation account, income
   statement   26
arbitration, dispute resolution   47
assessment of workers   35
asset-led marketing   **6**
assets, sale of   23
authority   37
autocratic leadership   **45**

B

bank loans   23, 24
batch production   **49**
below-the-line promotion   **14**
benchmarking   55
bonuses   42
Boston matrix   **11**–12
brand   **7**, 16
   enhancing   17
   global brands   17
   and price of a product   13, 17
   and promotional strategy   15, 17
brand image   16
   and added value   48
   and product design   57
   and unique selling point   17

branding, three types of   16
budgets   **21**
   benefits of   21
   drawbacks of   22
   purpose of   21–22
buffer stock   56
bureaucratic leadership   **45**
business angels   23
business hierarchy   37–39
buying habits of customers,
   technology identifying   20

C

capacity utilisation   **50–51**
   ways of improving   51
capital   22, 23
cash cows, Boston matrix   11, 12
cash flow   **24**
   link to product life cycle   10
   and overtrading   58
cash-flow forecast   **24**
   calculating   25
   constructing   24–25
   impact on business   25–26
   interpreting   25
   limitations of   26
cell production   **53**
centralised organisational
   structure   38
chain of command   37
coaching   34
collective bargaining   **47**
commission   42
competition   8
competitive pricing   **13**
competitors   9
computer-aided design (CAD)   52
computer-aided manufacture
   (CAM)   52
computerised stock control   55
consultation
   dispute resolution method   47
   non-financial incentive   43
continuous improvement   52
contract of employment   31, 46
contribution pricing   **13**

control within an organisation   37–38
corporate branding   16
corporation tax   27
cost of sales   **27**
costs of creating a product   8, 57
crowd funding   23
customer choice   16
customer loyalty   10, 18, 19
customer needs, meeting   6, 49, 53, 58
customer service   19, 49, 58

D

data mining, large costs of   20
debt factoring   24
decentralised organisational
   structure   38
decline stage of product life
   cycle   9, 10
delayering   **39**
delegation   38, 43, 45
democratic leadership   **45**
design mix   **8**, 57
digital media   20
diseconomies of scale   58, 69–70
   impact on business and
      stakeholders   59
dismissal   46
dispute resolution methods   47
distribution channels   15–16, 66–68
dividend   **23**
dogs, Boston matrix   11, 12

E

e-commerce, small businesses   58
e-tailing   20
economies of scale   **57–58**
   diseconomies of scale   58
   impact on business and
      stakeholders   59
   small firms   58–59
emotional marketing   **15**
employee motivation *see* motivation
employer-employee relations   **46**
   and equal opportunities   46
   impact on business and its
      stakeholders   47
   and trade unions   47

Index

employment contracts   31, 46
empowerment   **39**
   non-financial incentive   43
   and total quality management
     (TQM)   54
   versus control of the workforce
     39–40
equal opportunities   46
Equality Act (2010)   46
ethical sourcing   8
exam skills   61–62
expectancy theories of
   motivation   42
expenditure   **21**
extension strategies, product life
   cycle   9–10
external economies of scale   **57**–58
external finance   23
external recruitment   **32**

F
family and friends, source of
   finance   23
feedback, 360-degree   35
Fielder's contingency theory of
   leadership   45
finance   21–30
   budgeting   21–22
   cash-flow forecasting   24–26
   income statement   26–28
   ration analysis   29–30
   sources of   22–24
financial incentives, employee
   motivation   42–43
financial objective   **26**
fixed costs, reduction of   28
flat organisational structure   **38**
flexible hours/working   31
   non-financial incentive   43
flow production   **50**
forecasting cash-flow   24–26
four Ps of the marketing mix   6–7
   place   15–16
   price   12–14
   product   7–12
   promotion   14–15

function of a product   8, 57
funding *see* finance

G
gig economy   32
global brands   17
global marketing   **17**
glocalisation   17
goods business, marketing mix   18
grants   24
gross profit   **28**
gross profit margin   **29**
growth
   and economies of scale   57–58
   stage of product life cycle   8, 9, 10

H
Herzberg's two-factor theory of
   motivation   41–42
hierarchy of a business   **37**
hierarchy of needs, Maslow's
   motivational theory   40–41
homeworking   31
hot-desking   31
human relations theory of
   motivation, Mayo   40
human resources (HR)   30–48
   appraisal   35
   changes in working practices
     30–32
   employer-employee
     relationships   46–47
   management and leadership   44–46
   motivation   40–44
   new technology impact   31
   organisational design   37–40
   recruitment   32–34
   training   34–35
   workforce performance   35–37
   workforce planning   32
hygiene factors, Herzberg's theory of
   motivation   41

I
income statement   **26**
   calculating gross profit and net
     profit   28

increasing profit, methods of   28
   main components of   26–28
induction training   34, 35
industrial action   47
information technology (IT)   52
innovation   **57**
internal economies of scale   **57**
internal finance   **22–23**
internal recruitment   **32**
internet
   e-tailing   20
   promotion via   14
interviews, recruitment   33
introduction stage of product life
   cycle   8, 9, 10

J
job analysis   33
job description   33
job enlargement   43
job enrichment   43
job production   **49**
job rotation   34
   non-financial incentive   43
job satisfaction   41, 42
job-sharing   31
job-specific training   34
just-in-case stock control   55
just-in-time (JIT) stock
   management   **53**, 55

K
Kaizen   **52**

L
labour productivity   **35**–36
labour turnover   **36**
   internal and external factors   36
   negative and positive effects
     of   36–37
   questions and answers   72–74
laissez-faire leadership style   45
large global business, marketing
   mix   18
large national business, marketing
   mix   18

lead time **56**
leadership
  styles 45
  theories 45–46
lean production **52**
  benefits of 53
  drawbacks of 53
  techniques of 52–53
leasing 24
life cycle of a product 8–11
living wage 46
loans 23, 24

M

m-commerce 20
management layers, large versus small firms 59
management by objectives 44, 70–72
management styles, McGregor 44
managerial economies of scale 57
margin, profit 29–30
market growth, Boston matrix 11, 12
market orientation **6**
market share, Boston matrix 11, 12
market structure business, marketing mix 19
marketing **6**
marketing mix **6**–7
  decisions about 16–19
  in different contexts 18–19
  effect of new technology 20
  four Ps of 6–16
marketing strategies **17**
Maslow's hierarchy of needs theory of motivation 40–41
mass market business, marketing mix 19
matrix organisational structure **39**
maturity stage of product life cycle 9, 10
maximum stock level 56
Mayo's human relations theory of motivation 40

McGregor's theory X and theory Y, management style 44
minimum wage 46
monitoring, total quality management 54
MOPS (market, objectives, product, situation) 62
motivation 40–44
  effect of poor 58
  financial and non-financial methods of 42–43, 64–66
  impact of motivated workforce 43–44
  and productivity 50
  theories of 40–43
motivators 41
multi-channel distribution 16
multi-skilling **30**
multinational corporations 17

N

narrow span of control **37**
needs, Maslow's motivational theory 40–41
negotiation, dispute resolution 47
net cash flow 25
net profit **28**
net profit margin 29–30
new technology, impact on working practices 31
niche market business, marketing mix 19
non-financial incentives, employee motivation 43

O

objectives
  financial 26
  management by 44
off-the-job training **34**
on-the-job training **34**
online distribution 16
online sales 13
operating profit 27, 63–64
operations management 48–60
  added value 48–49

economies of scale 57–59
lean production 52–53
production methods 49–50
productivity 50–51
purchasing 55–57
quality 54–55
research and development (R&D) 57
technology 52
organisational design 37–40
overdrafts 24
overhead costs 27
overstocking 57
overtrading 58
owner's capital, source of finance 22

P

part-time staff 30
paternalistic leadership **45**
peer assessment 35
peer-to-peer funding 23
penetration pricing **12**
performance-related pay 43
performance of workers 35–37
person specification 33
personal branding 16
piece rate **40**
place, marketing mix 15–16
Porter and Lawler's expectancy theory of motivation 42
portfolio analysis, Boston matrix 11–12
price skimming **12**
pricing strategies 12–14
problem children, Boston matrix 11, 12
producer **15**
  distribution channels 15–16
product 7
product branding 16
product design 57
product design mix 8
product differentiation 7
  and survival of small firms 58
product extension strategies 9–10

product life cycle **8**–9
  benefits   11
  and cash flow   10
  diagram   9
  drawbacks   11
  examples   10
  and extension strategies   9–10
  stages of   8–9
product orientation   6
product portfolio   **7**
  Boston matrix analysis   11–12
production   **49**
  and economies of scale   57–58
  lean   52–53
  methods of   49–50
productivity   50
  capacity utilisation   50–51
  of labour   35–36
  and leadership   45
  and motivation   40, 42–43
  ways of improving   50
profit
  calculation of   26
  gross profit   28
  gross profit margin   29
  net profit   28
  net profit margin   29–30
  ratio analysis   29–30
  retained   23
  ways of improving   28
profit and loss account, income
  statement   26
profit sharing   42
profitability   29
promotion   14–15
promotional mix   14
psychological pricing   **13**
public relations (PR)   15
'pull' system of production   53
purchasing   55–57
purchasing economies of scale   57

Q

quality   54
quality assurance   **54**

quality chain, teams in TQM   54
quality circles   **54**
quality control   **54**

R

ratio analysis   29–30
recruitment and selection   **32**
  employee selection methods   33
  importance of recruitment
    33–34
  internal and external
    recruitment   32
  job analysis, job description and
    person specification   33
reorder level, stock control   56
research and development
  (R&D)   **57**
  and external economies of
    scale   58
resource depletion, concerns
  over   8
responsibility   37
  and leadership   44
  and quality   54
  and worker motivation   41, 43
retailer   **15–16**
retained profits, internal source of
  finance   23
revenue
  income statement   26–28
  and profitability calculations
    28, 29
rising stars, Boston matrix   11, 12
robotics   52

S

sales
  cost of   27
  increasing   28
sales of assets, internal finance   23
saturation stage of product life
  cycle   9
scientific management, Taylor's
  (motivational) theory   40
selection exercises   33

selection of staff see recruitment
  and selection
self-assessment   35
services business, marketing mix   19
share capital   **23**
share ownership   43
shareholders   8, 23, 26–27
skills see training
small firms
  marketing mix   18
  survival of   58
SMART objectives   44
social media   14, 17, 20
social trends   8, 16
span of control   37
specialisation   57
sponsorship   15
stakeholders   8
stock   55
stock control   **55**
  just-in-time (JIT) management   53
  questions and answers   76–78
stock-control diagram   **55–56**
stock level   56
stock out   56
suppliers
  and purchasing   55
  relocation and economies of
    scale   58
  and stock control   56
  and trade credit   24

T

tall organisational structure   **38**
Taylor's theory of scientific
  management   40
teamwork
  cell production   53
  matrix organisational
    structure   39
  non-financial incentive   43
  total quality management
    (TQM)   54
technical economies of scale   57
technology   52
  impact on working practices   31

use of by marketing   20
telephone interviews   33
temporary staff   31
testing (of job applicants)   33
theory X and theory Y,
    McGregor   44
time-based management   53
total quality management
    (TQM)   **54**
trade credit   24
trade disputes   47
trade unions   **47**
trading account, income
    statement   26
training   34–35
    importance of   35
    multi-skilling   30
    and productivity   50
transnational corporations   17
turnover of labour

calculation of   36
internal and external factors
    affecting   36
negative and positive effects
    of   36–37
two-factor theory of motivation,
    Herzberg   41–42

U
unique selling point (USP)   **7**, 13
    small firms   58

V
value, added   7, 48–49
variable costs, reduction of   28
venture capital   **23**
viral marketing   **14**
Vroom's expectancy theory of
    motivation   42

W
waste management, design
    issues   8
waste minimisation question   79–81
waste reduction, lean production
    methods   52–53
wholesaler   **15**
wide span of control   **37**
WJEC exam structure   61
work trials   33
workforce performance   35–37
workforce planning   32
working patterns, impact of changes
    in   31–32
Wright and Taylor's theory of
    leadership   46

Z
zero defects, total quality
    management   54
zero-hours contracts   31